THE LAST DAYS OF
STONEWALL JACKSON

by Chris Mackowski and Kristopher D. White

Kris: For Donna and Evan, who never gave up on a son's dream.

Chris: For Stephwall and Jackson, my "little comforters."

We jointly dedicate this book to our friend and mentor, Frank O'Reilly.

ACKNOWLEDGEMENTS

We appreciate the support of our colleagues at Fredericksburg & Spotsylvania National Military Park, especially John Hennessy, Greg Mertz, Eric Mink, Don Pfanz, Janice Frye, and Noel Harrison, who all made contributions to this volume. We especially thank Frank O'Reilly for his editorial work, inspiration, and more. We also thank Ray Castner, Joe Haydon, and Jim Goode.

At St. Bonaventure University's Russell J. Jandoli School of Journalism and Mass Communication, we thank Denny Wilkins and John Hanchette. Thanks, too, to the dean, Lee Coppola, whose behind-the-scenes support and encouragement have made much of this project possible. A special "wave of the arm" to Patrick Vecchio for his editing and encouragement.

We offer our appreciation to Colonel Keith Gibson of the Virginia Military Institute, whose stewardship of Jackson remains stalwart and keen. The photo of Little Sorrel appears courtesy of VMI.

The photo of the Reverend Lacy appears courtesy of the Presbyterian Church of Fredericksburg. *Portrait of Beverly Tucker Lacy* (undated) by James Reeve Stuart appears courtesy of Washington and Lee University, Lexington, Virginia.

Thanks to John Cummings and the Friends of Fredericksburg Area Battlefields for supporting this publication and to Jackson Foster of The ID Entity for the handsome design work.

Finally—and most importantly—we offer our thanks to our families: to Sarah White and to Heidi, Stephanie, and Jackson Mackowski.

CONTENTS

FORWORD

There is a timelessness about heroes and legends. They
can transcend time and space, and are almost prescient in
everything they do.

Lieutenant General Thomas J. "Stonewall" Jackson
certainly had that special quality that brought hope to a
generation of Confederates in the 1860's—and provided an
inspiration that has resonated with every generation of Americans ever since. General George S. Patton admitted that as a
boy, he learned to pray while two portraits of bearded figures
watched over him. Early on Patton concluded that they must
be God and his son, Jesus Christ. Only later did he learn that
God was actually Robert E. Lee, and the Christ-like figure
was "Stonewall" Jackson. Somehow, it still made perfect sense
to the general. Similarly, the commandant of the U.S. Marine
Corps, and Medal of Honor recipient, General Alexander
Archer Vandegrift, recalled praying with his grandfather, a
Baptist deacon who did not care much for men or mankind.
But those that he did respect, he held in high esteem—as he
insisted on praying every day to the God of Abraham and
Isaac, and of Robert E. Lee and "Stonewall" Jackson. Thomas
J. "Stonewall" Jackson had earned a reputation as a tenacious
soldier, but he was also remembered as a pious, devout
Christian. The combination transformed a shy, introverted
professor from Lexington, Virginia, into an almost messianic
symbol for the Confederacy and a pillar of the Lost Cause
interpretation of the Civil War. Jackson's ideals and actions
certainly made an impact on America and the way Americans
perceive themselves.

Lieutenant General Thomas Jonathan "Stonewall" Jackson
reached the pinnacle of his career at the very moment he was
cut down tragically in the mistaken fire of his own men on
May 2, 1863. In the course of two years, he had rocketed from

near obscurity to become an American folk hero. Jackson had become the living embodiment of what Horatio Alger later styled the Self-Made Man. He was the common clay made good, and he still serves as a role model for many today who study his personal as well as his martial virtues.

The death of Jackson sent shockwaves throughout the Confederacy. When Lee heard the news, he confessed, "I know not how to replace him." Confederate President Jefferson Davis called the general's demise "a great national calamity." Peter Alexander of the *Southern Literary Messenger* eulogized Jackson: "He is the idol of the people, and is the object of greater enthusiasm than any other military chieftain of our day." Soldiers and civilians agreed. A member of the 21st Georgia wrote, "A greater hero never lived…. If we could only see Jackson, we was all right." An Englishman noted that "the sight of him, and of him alone, stirred the blood like a trumpet, and the words 'Stonewall is coming' carried confidence to his friends and terror to his foes." And sometimes, just the thought of him, sight unseen, inspired soldiers. A young Missouri captain, Norval Spangler, fell mortally wounded in a distant battle at Champion's Hill, Mississippi, on May 16, 1863, shortly after news of Jackson's death had been reported. Spangler announced, "I guess I'll take supper with Stonewall Jackson tonight." So many worthy Confederate officers had fallen in the West, but Spangler, and his nation, fixated on the Virginian who had died at Guiney Station. A matronly diarist from Winchester lamented in her journal: "'The Mighty has fallen,' but he carries to his grave the hopes, and is followed by the bitter tears of the people in whose defense he lost his life, and who loved him with grateful devotion." Cornelia McDonald concluded, "No loss could be felt as his will be."

In short, Thomas J. Jackson's untimely death was deeply affecting for many who knew him and countless more who knew only of him. Southerners obviously mourned their general. But so did a surprising number of Northerners and much of the English-speaking world. Union soldiers sought out veteran officers of the Old Army to hear tales of

Stonewall Jackson in better days. *The Philadelphia Press* lamented the death of the great captain, even though he fought for the Confederacy. President Abraham Lincoln wrote to the editor, John W. Forney, to thank him for his appropriate words and express his own admiration for Jackson, calling him "a gallant man."

British newspapers lionized the fallen Stonewall with an unexpected degree of empathy. *The Times of London* reflected: "even on this side of the ocean the gallant soldier's fate will everywhere be heard of with pity and sympathy, not only as a brave man…but as one of the consummate generals that this century has produced," instantly elevating him into an elite category with the likes of Napoleon and their own Duke of Wellington. "Stonewall Jackson," *The Times* concluded, "will carry with him to his early grave the regrets of all who can admire greatness and genius." An English admirer wrote at the time: "It was impossible to look at the house where he lay…without a mist coming over the eyes and a choking sense of suffocation rising in the throat."

But it would be a mistake to look at Jackson as merely a dead relic of a bygone era or a piece of "Lost Cause" iconography. Stonewall Jackson left a profound legacy for generations well beyond his own. Jackson's severe piety and quirky personality made him a noteworthy character, but it was his military genius that makes Stonewall as relevant today as he was in 1863.

Modern warriors still hearken back to the Civil War and Stonewall Jackson to find precedents for grand strategy. George S. Patton once assured Dwight D. Eisenhower: "I will be your Jackson." Generals Douglas MacArthur, Alexander A. Vandegrift, Holland M. "Howling Mad" Smith, and the colorful Lewis B. "Chesty" Puller all drew lessons and inspiration from the legendary Jackson. The U.S. Eighth Army's commander, General Robert L. Eichelberger, remembered MacArthur telling him he wanted "me to become a Stonewall Jackson." Chesty Puller literally adopted Stonewall as his hero and embraced his credo: "Never take counsel of your fears." Puller carried a dog-eared copy of G. F. R. Henderson's

"IT WOULD BE A MISTAKE TO LOOK AT JACKSON AS MERELY A DEAD RELIC OF A BYGONE ERA OR A PIECE OF 'LOST CAUSE' ICONOGRAPHY."

biography of Jackson throughout his campaigns from Guadalcanal to Korea. Stonewall Jackson could touch the heart and the mind, as well as the soul of a soldier.

Christopher Mackowski and Kristopher White have written an outstanding analysis of Lieutenant General Thomas J. Jackson's last days on the Chandler plantation at Guiney Station. These two fine historians have put this enduring tale in context with history, romance, legend, and the legacy of the Lost Cause. They have culled through an impressive array of primary and secondary source materials. Their interpretation of Stonewall Jackson's last days in the America of 1863 is fair-minded, balanced, and revealing. Readers, whether Jackson scholars or those learning about the general for the first time, will find this study both illuminating and entertaining.

I hope readers will not only learn about a great man and great soldier who wove a vital thread through the tapestry of American history, but will also find inspiration to visit the sites that Stonewall Jackson made famous and which, in turn, made Stonewall famous.

—Francis Augustín O'Reilly

Civil War historian and author of *The Fredericksburg Campaign: Winter War on the Rappahannock*, and *"Stonewall" Jackson at Fredericksburg*.

May 11th, 1863.

General Order 61 Hdqrs. Army of Northern Virginia.

With deep grief, the commanding general announces to the army the death of

Lt. Gen. T. J. Jackson, who expired on the 10th inst, at 3:15 PM. The daring, skill, and energy

of this great and good soldier, by the decree of an all-wise Providence, are now lost to us.

But while we mourn his death, we feel that his spirit still lives, and will inspire the whole army

with his indomitable courage and unshaken confidence in God as our hope and strength.

Let his name be a watchword to his corps, who have followed him to victory on so many fields.

Let officers and soldiers emulate his invincible determination to do everything in the defense

of our beloved country.

R.E. Lee

General.

CHAPTER ONE

THE ATTACK

—◆—

Saturday, May 2, 1863

On May 2, 1863, Jackson's men stormed out of the woods and overran the Union line.

Lieutenant General Thomas Jonathan "Stonewall" Jackson surveyed his men, some twenty-eight thousand of them—ready, like a hammer, to slam into the unsuspecting Union flank.

They had spent all day marching, four abreast, over dirt roads that wound hidden through the Wilderness of Spotsylvania. There had been only one bit of trouble, back at Catharine Furnace, but it was nothing the men of the 23rd Georgia hadn't been able to take care of while the rest of the column slipped away on a road so freshly cut it remained as yet unmapped. The column's guide, Charles Wellford, knew of the road because his family owned the iron furnace: that area was his home.

The rest of the march, conducted in near silence to preserve its secrecy, remained uneventful.

At three, Jackson scribbled a quick note to his commander, General Robert E. Lee: "General, The enemy has made a stand at Chancellors's which is about 2 miles from Chancellorsville. I hope as soon as practicable to attack. I trust that an Ever Kind Providence will bless us with great success."

Lee, with fourteen thousand men, had remained east of the Union army, acting as a diversion while Jackson's men marched into position. Jackson would be the hammer, Lee the anvil, and the Union army would be trapped between—trapped, then smashed.

That the Union right flank dangled unprotected, so ripe for his hammer blow, seemed providential to Jackson. Major

The intersection where Lee and Jackson sat down for their "Crackerbox Meeting" on the evening of May 1 (which is pictured below). The two generals also met briefly there on the morning of May 2 as Jackson's column set off on its flank march.

General Jeb Stuart, the commander of Lee's cavalry, had brought the news to Lee and Jackson the night before as the two generals, sitting on a pair of cracker boxes around a campfire, had been discussing their options. They knew the Army of the Potomac drastically outnumbered them but had no way to know just how badly—more than two to one. Despite the numbers, Lee had used his smaller army on that first day to strike his unsuspecting foe. The Union commander, Major General Joseph Hooker, responded by withdrawing his army into a defensive position. Lee, ever audacious, wanted to seize the initiative Hooker had relinquished—he just needed a place to strike.

Stuart provided the exact piece of intelligence Lee needed: The Union right flank lay exposed and unprotected. Lee sent Stuart to gather additional information then turned to Jackson, and the two men began to formulate a plan. Jackson would march his entire corps—twenty-eight thousand men— around to attack the unprotected Union flank.

Just after sunrise on May 2, the lead brigades of Jackson's "Foot Cavalry" started out on what would be their greatest march.

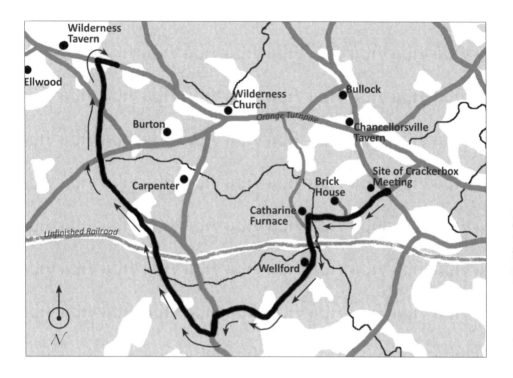

Route of Jackson's flank attack.

Now, nearly ten hours later, those men stood in a line of battle nearly a mile and a half long. "Who could not conquer with troops such as these," Jackson had once said of his men. Now, as he surveyed them from his perch atop his favorite horse, Little Sorrel, he felt similar pride in what they had accomplished—and what they were about to.

A third of his men still remained on the march. Jackson couldn't afford to wait for them, he decided. Little more than two hours of sunlight remained. He would launch the attack with the two divisions already in place and the third division, General A.P. Hill's, would come in later as the reserve. That gave Jackson nearly twenty-eight thousand men in all.

A retinue of officers and staff members surrounded Jackson, awaiting the order to begin. Jackson looked at them—so many familiar faces, so many of them former students and colleagues from his pre-war days at the Virginia Military Institute. His time in Lexington, teaching at VMI, had been the happiest ten years of his life. Since then, he had risen from a relatively obscure college professor to become one of the

most famous military figures in the world. Those Lexington days seemed a lifetime ago. Yet among the men with him today, ready to execute one of the boldest military maneuvers of the war, he had seventeen comrades from those bygone days, including the two division commanders who would launch the attack, Generals Robert Rodes and Raleigh Colston. "The Institute will be heard from today," Jackson said.

Minutes passed. Couriers brought information and went away with orders. The final pieces were snapping into place.

Jackson pulled his overcoat tighter to him. Although the temperature had probably reached into the mid-80s that afternoon, he still felt a chill, had been feeling it for a day or two. Sleeping on the ground the night before hadn't helped.

He consulted his watch: 5:15 p.m.

Time.

"Are you ready, General Rodes?" Jackson asked.

"Yes, sir," Rodes answered.

"You may move forward then."

*   *   *   *   *

The Union Eleventh Corps, posted at the far end of the Federal line, had settled in for a quiet evening. Positioned well away from the day's fighting, they didn't even expect to get called in as reserves. Soldiers had stacked their arms, and many of them had begun to cook dinner.

Word had come to them earlier in the day about a possible Confederate retreat across their front. The thick underbrush made it impossible to see much of anything, but pickets facing south did their best to keep a lookout.

Far fewer eyes faced west.

In fact, Major General Oliver Otis Howard, commander of the Eleventh Corps, had positioned only two regiments and two artillery pieces to face westward down the Plank Road, some nine hundred men in all, as token protection for the Union flank—but with all the fighting happening on the eastern front beyond the Chancellor house, some three miles away, few seriously expected anything to happen here.

The thickness of Spotsylvania's wilderness not only masked but also muffled the approach of Jackson's men. When Jackson gave his order to advance and the bugles sounded out, the Union soldiers heard nothing through the foliage. The first clue they had of anything amiss came when deer, rabbits, and other game—driven ahead of the Confederate advance—suddenly darted out of the forest.

"Following the bugles were a few scattering shots," wrote Henry Kyd Douglas, the youngest member of Jackson's staff, "and then from the opening in the road, the whiz of shell and, following after the wild game escaping from the wood, 'Jackson's Foot Cavalry' were upon them. The gray line moved on regularly with the whoop and yell and the rattle of musketry. There was, there could be, no effective attempt at resistance."

The Confederate attack swept the Union Eleventh Corps from the field, driving them eastward under an unrelenting tide. "They did run and make no mistake about it," wrote Lieutenant Octavis Wiggins of the 37th North Carolina infantry. "But I will never blame them. I would have done the same thing and so would you and I reckon the Devil himself would have run with Jackson in his rear."

Not all Union resistance instantly crumbled, though. Many units of the Eleventh Corps put up a brave, if brief, fight. A New York colonel, Adolphus Bushbeck, threw together a thin blue line and made a stand along the Plank Road near the Wilderness Church, holding up a portion of the Confederate attack. Federals then put up a secondary line a few miles farther east.

Elsewhere, the 8th Pennsylvania Cavalry was caught between the Confederate skirmish line and the main Confederate battle line. The Pennsylvanians had to cut their way to freedom, but only after sustaining heavy losses of men and horses. That particular engagement would have haunting repercussions later in the evening.

Jackson's men eventually overran any such pockets of resistance, but the resulting hold-ups meant some portions of the Confederate line advanced farther and faster than others.

"...THE ENEMY HAS MADE A STAND AT CHANCELLORS'S WHICH IS ABOUT 2 MILES FROM CHANCELLORSVILLE. I HOPE AS SOON AS PRACTICABLE TO ATTACK. I TRUST THAT AN EVER KIND PROVIDENCE WILL BLESS US WITH GREAT SUCCESS."

—Stonewall Jackson's last dispatch to Robert E. Lee

The sudden appearance of Confederates took many Union soldiers unawares. Most of them had been cooking dinner and relaxing when the Confederates attacked.

The terrain also hampered Confederate progress. The dense undergrowth, thick with thorns and vines, made a shoulder-to-shoulder advance in line of battle virtually impossible. The dips, swales, and hillocks of the ground made it worse.

"Press on! Press on!" Jackson urged. But eventually, the tangled Confederate line could press no farther.

*　　*　　*　　*　　*

That Jackson had come this far at all—on this day or in this life—demonstrated how tenaciously he followed his own credo: "You may be whatever you resolve to be."

Jackson's resolve had propelled him to his current position—one of most renowned military men in the world in the middle of one of his most daring maneuvers—from modest beginnings. Born in what was then western Virginia, in the town of Clarksburg, Jackson was left orphaned by the age of six and raised by an uncle. His only other family, a younger sister, Laura, was sent north to live with other relatives.

Growing up, Jackson developed a strict work ethic—strong enough to eventually overcome his lack of formal education. At age eighteen, he received an appointment to West Point, where he was woefully under-prepared for the rigorous academic curriculum. Through intensive study, though, he managed to finish his first semester ranked seventy-first out of 101 cadets. Over the next three years, Jackson continued to focus all of his considerable willpower on his studies, and his academic standing steadily rose. By the time he graduated, he ranked seventeenth out of fifty-nine, and one classmate speculated that if he and his classmates had to attend school for a fifth year, Jackson might have worked his way to top of the class—an amazing feat since many historians consider the Class of 1846 the greatest West Point would ever produce.

Jackson's class graduated just as the United States declared war on Mexico. Jackson received a commission as a second lieutenant in the artillery, and he took part in the American expeditionary force that drove inland from the Gulf coast and captured Mexico City. Jackson earned commendations for gallantry and was breveted to major. It was during his time in Mexico that Jackson also awakened to religion, which would grow to become the dominant force in his life.

A short army career after the war proved unfulfilling, especially when a longstanding quarrel erupted with a fellow officer. In 1851, Jackson resigned to take a post at VMI teaching Natural and Experimental Philosophy—better known today as physics—and artillery tactics. He was not, it turned out, well-suited to teaching, and his first few years in the classroom proved difficult for Jackson and his students. On the artillery field, however, Jackson excelled.

"Of all places…" Jackson said of his new hometown, "this little village is the most beautiful." As he settled into the Lexington community, he became a deacon at his Presbyterian church. He also established a Sunday school for blacks and taught them to read the Bible—an act that violated Virginia law, which forbade slaves from learning how to read. Everyone deserved access to the Word of God, Jackson resolved.

Jackson married twice during his years in Lexington. His first wife, Ellie Junkin, a Presbyterian minister's daughter, died giving birth to a stillborn son after only fourteen months of marriage. When Jackson married again, he again married a minister's daughter, Mary Anna Morrison. The newlyweds bought a home in Lexington, a two-story brick house on East Washington Street. A year after they married, the couple had a daughter, Mary Graham, who died only a few weeks after birth.

From this simple, undistinguished life, Jackson would rise to worldwide prominence. He first made himself noticed, and earned his distinctive nickname "Stonewall," at the first battle of Manassas in July of 1861. Ordered to hold a hilltop position near the center of the crumbling Confederate line, Jackson's men provided a rallying point that shifted the tide of battle. "Yonder stands Jackson like a stone wall," cried a Confederate general. "Let us go to his assistance." Countless retellings over time evolved those words into a legendary rallying cry, carved

Jackson's home on East Washington Street in Lexington.

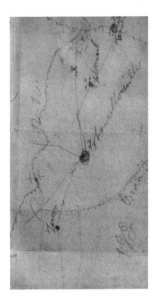

Jackson carried this rough map that sketched out the area around Chancellorsville.

into marble for the ages: "There stands Jackson like a stone wall. Rally around the Virginians!"

The Confederate victory at Manassas would be the first in a string of military achievements for Jackson. The following spring, his movements in the Shenandoah Valley—what would later become known as Jackson's Valley Campaign—would see his men march more than 600 miles between late March and early June, fighting six battles against three Union armies that outnumbered his forces at least three to one. He lost only one battle—the first, because of faulty intelligence from his cavalry—and he never lost again. His men would earn the nickname "Jackson's Foot Cavalry" for their ability to cover so much ground so quickly. Most importantly, at a time when the Confederacy suffered setback after setback on nearly every front, Jackson's brilliant maneuvers in the Valley turned him into a national hero. "His name alone is worth ten thousand men," a Union soldier would later write.

In subsequent months, Jackson would earn a place as one of Robert E. Lee's most trusted subordinates. When Lee reorganized the Army of Northern Virginia in November of 1862, he placed General James Longstreet at the head of the First Corps; at the head of the Second, he placed Jackson. Lee used the Second Corps as the quick-strike part of his army, specializing in fast, surprise maneuvers. Lee, ever an aggressive strategist, found in Jackson the perfect tactician to execute his plans. What Lee resolved, Jackson carried out.

And that had made Jackson the ideal man to lead the flank attack at Chancellorsville.

*　　*　　*　　*　　*

Now, nearly four hours into that flank attack, with his momentum gone and his men in disarray, Jackson halted the advance.

But only momentarily.

His third division, under A.P. Hill, had finally arrived and was getting into position. Jackson intended to send Hill's men forward to resume the offensive, giving Colston and Rodes the time they needed to reform.

Daylight had faded to twilight, and twilight to darkness. A full moon lifted itself above the forest, though little of its light could penetrate the thick foliage.

A night attack would be risky, Jackson knew, but waiting would be riskier. If he gave the Federals the opportunity to dig in, then his men would have to assault fortified positions in the morning. He resolved to press his advantage now, while the Union army was still reeling. If he succeeded, he might even be able to sever the Union army's route of retreat.

To better assess his situation, Jackson decided to do a bit of reconnaissance. He sent out word that he needed a guide, and soon Private David Joseph Kyle of the 9th Virginia Cavalry came forward. Kyle knew the area well: He lived on the Bullock Road, less than a quarter of a mile from their current position, so this was literally his back yard.

The Mountain Road circa the mid-1880s.

Rather than take Jackson down the Plank Road, an exposed route well-lit by the moonlight, Kyle led Jackson and his seven-man party toward a road that didn't show up on any maps. The Mountain Road, as it was called, had once been the main road through the area but had since fallen into general disuse since the turnpike had been put in. It ran, like a dark tunnel through the trees, for a little less than two miles on a course roughly parallel to the Plank Road.

Passing through the line of the 18th North Carolina, Jackson's party rode about two hundred yards forward. Ahead of them another twenty yards, the 33rd North Carolina stretched out in a skirmish line; another 250 yards beyond the North Carolinians waited the Federals. From that direction, Jackson could hear trees falling and earth being moved. The Federals were digging in.

Jackson turned Little Sorrel around and led his men back toward the main Confederate line.

They were only ninety yards away when, from the south, thunder rolled up the Confederate line and the forest in front of Jackson exploded with fire.

CHAPTER TWO

THE WOUNDING

— ◆ —

Saturday, May 2, 1863

Despite the light of the full moon that night, Jackson and his staff were shrouded by the thick darkness of the Wilderness when his men accidentally opened fire on him.

Several hundred yards to the south, a Pennsylvania unit, the 128th Infantry, had stumbled quite by accident into the main Confederate line. Its appearance discomfited the Confederates all the more because it seemed the Pennsylvanians had somehow slipped past the skirmishers that had been posted forward. Realizing their blunder, the Pennsylvanians tried to escape, but the Confederates took a large number of them prisoner.

Word of the incident spread along the Confederate line: Union troops wandering through the darkness were liable to appear at any time and at any place.

Already skittish, Confederates began shooting at shadows. One jumpy Confederate would infect the man next to him. The shooting intensified and, like a wave, began moving northward along the entire Confederate line.

It rolled across Jackson's front just as he and his men returned down the Mountain Road from their reconnaissance mission.

"Cease firing!" yelled Lieutenant Joseph Morrison, Jackson's brother-in-law and staff officer, who had his horse shot out from under him by the initial volley. "You are firing into your own men!"

A veteran unit, the 18th North Carolinians had heard it all. They knew the tricks. And, after all, hadn't the 8th Pennsylvania Cavalry been caught behind Confederate lines just a couple hours earlier? Hadn't Union units been captured wandering around lost between the lines? And weren't these horsemen—probably cavalrymen—coming from the direction of the Union lines?

"It's a lie!" responded Major John Barry. "Pour it into them, boys!"

By this time, the North Carolinians had had time to reload. They cut loose with the power of a full, concentrated volley.

The darkness and density of the forest protected most of Jackson's men. One fell dead, another wounded, but the others escaped unscathed—except for Jackson himself. Three bullets struck him: one in the right hand, one in the left forearm, and one three inches below the left shoulder.

Little Sorrel bolted in panic. Jackson, barely able to stay on, held up a hand to protect himself as the horse plowed through the underbrush. A thick branch hit Jackson in the face, nearly knocking him to the ground. With effort, he began to rein in Little Sorrel enough so that his staffers could come to his aid.

As they tried to ease him from his saddle, Jackson collapsed onto one of his men. They then lowered him the rest of the way and began to attend to him. Little Sorrel, still panicked, tore away again, bolting eastward through the forest. Riderless, he would gallop through the Union line and be captured.

Jackson was not the only general caught in the cascading musketry. Out on the Plank Road, which ran parallel to the Mountain Road less than thirty yards to the south, A. P. Hill had gone forward with a reconnaissance party of his own. His nine men, far more exposed on the wider road and well-lit by the full moon, were all killed or wounded or had their horses panic and bolt toward the Federal line. Hill, untouched, survived by diving to the ground.

Hill quickly recovered and was among the first on the scene to help Jackson. He and Captain Richard Wilbourn pulled off Jackson's gloves, stripped away his heavy India-rubber raincoat, and tore open his sleeves to examine the wounds. They applied bandages, made a sling for the left arm, and waited for help to arrive.

*   *   *   *   *

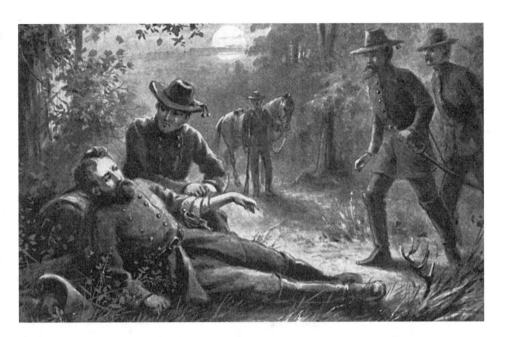

The firing along the Confederate line had not gone unnoticed by the Federals, who soon opened up an artillery bombardment now that they had an approximate idea of the Confederate position. One Federal gun unlimbered in the middle of the Plank Road only a few hundred yards away from the fallen Jackson.

As if to underscore the proximity of the enemy, two Union soldiers wandered into the small clearing where attendants were bandaging the general's wounds. Before they could take in the situation, Confederate soldiers took them prisoner. Where there were two Union soldiers, might there not be more? Jackson's staff members quickly decided it was time to move.

As they tried to carry him away from the front, Jackson worried that news of his wounding would impact the morale of his men. He asked that his condition be kept secret. "When asked, just say it is a Confederate officer," he instructed. Curiosity seekers from the ranks abounded.

Soon, a litter party arrived. They laid Jackson on the stretcher, hoisted him to shoulder height, and began to move more quickly.

Moments after Confederate fire felled his own scouting party, Gen. A.P. Hill rushed to the aid of Jackson. Command devolved onto Hill, but he had to surrender it shortly thereafter when he sustained wounds in both legs.

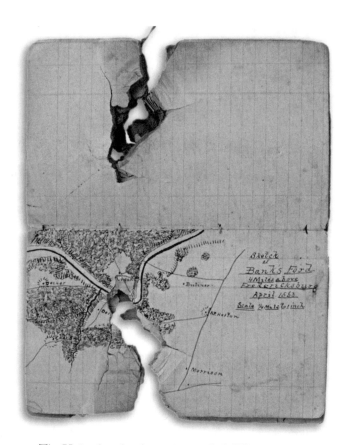

One of Jackson's engineers, Capt. Keith Boswell, was killed by the same burst of fire that wounded Jackson. Boswell's sketchbook shows the ravages of the bullet that killed him.

The Union bombardment intensified. "The whole atmosphere seemed filled with whistling canister and shrieking shell, tearing the trees on every side," Morrison later wrote. The litter party moved less than fifty yards when a piece of flying metal hit one of the lead stretcher bearers, forcing him to drop the front left corner of the litter, pitching Jackson to the ground from shoulder height. Jackson landed on his wounded shoulder.

After waiting out the artillery fire for a few minutes, Jackson's staffers scooped him up and carried him away. Soon, they recruited enough men for a second litter party. As they pushed through the thick underbrush, one of the bearers became entangled in a grape vine and tripped, dumping the litter again.

The initial gunshot wounds, while painful, had not caused an excessive amount of bleeding. Now, as the result of one of

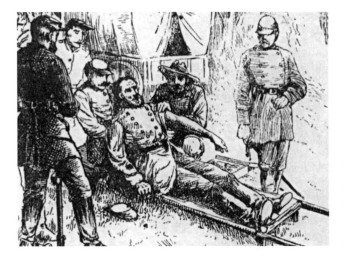

After carrying Jackson part way out of the woods, his men were eventually able to load him onto an ambulance that could take him to safety.

the litter accidents, the artery in Jackson's left shoulder began to hemorrhage.

Things looked more grim than ever. A renewed urgency gripped Jackson's men. They again placed him on the litter and carried him a few hundred yards. In their wake, word spread among the men of Jackson's command that some terrible accident had befallen their leader in the dark woods of the Wilderness.

"Engulfed in the midst of that gloomy thicket, surrounded with so much suffering and death, with the mournful and continuous cry of the plaintive whippoorwill, made the scene inexpressibly sad," wrote Colonel W. L. Goldsmith of Thomas's Georgia brigade, "and to many the poor night-birds seemed to be piping the funeral notes of the Confederacy's death."

*   *   *   *   *

Dr. Hunter McGuire had been riding near the front, "anxious to remove the wounded from the field" before it got too late, when a courier arrived. He whispered to McGuire the news about Jackson's wounding and said the general needed him. McGuire set out at once.

McGuire, then only twenty-seven years old, had already earned a reputation as one of the finest surgeons in the Army

Dr. Hunter Holmes McGuire, Jackson's chief medical officer.

of Northern Virginia. Born in Winchester, Virginia, in October, 1835, McGuire graduated from medical school at age twenty. For a short time, he practiced medicine in his hometown with his father, but his heart lay in the classroom. He gave up his share of the medical practice for a teaching career, which took him first to Philadelphia and then, when sectional tensions become too hot, to Richmond and New Orleans.

He was in the Crescent City when hostilities between North and South broke out, so he returned to Virginia and enlisted as a private in the 2nd Virginia Infantry. However, because of the scarcity of doctors, his talent as a surgeon quickly won him a commission in the Medical Department. In May of 1861, Virginia's governor assigned McGuire to serve as the chief medical officer for the Army of the Shenandoah, then headquartered at Harpers Ferry under the command of Thomas Jonathan Jackson.

"You look like a young man," Jackson had said to McGuire at their first meeting.

"I am a young man," the young doctor replied.

The two conversed cordially, then Jackson told the doctor to report back to his quarters until Jackson called for him. McGuire waited a week. Jackson, meanwhile, inquired with Richmond whether a mistake had been made. Finally assured that McGuire was, indeed, the right man, Jackson accepted him into the fold. The two became fast friends.

Now, McGuire quickly rode to the aid of his friend and commander. On the way, he encountered other members of Jackson's inner circle, mapmaker Jed Hotchkiss and Major Alexander "Sandie" Pendleton, Jackson's chief of staff. Rumors also reached them—rumors that Jackson had been taken prisoner, that Confederate troops were falling back in disorder.

"At this moment poor Sandy, overwhelmed with grief, fell from his horse, fainting," McGuire said. McGuire administered medicinal whiskey, gave instructions to Hotchkiss, then set off to find Jackson.

McGuire found Jackson near the side of the road, still on the litter. He looked at Jackson with concern. "I hope you are not badly hurt, General," he said.

"I am badly injured, Doctor; I fear I am dying," Jackson replied, calmly but feebly. "I am glad you have come. I think the wound in my shoulder is still bleeding."

Indeed, it was. "His clothes were saturated with blood, and hemorrhage was still going on from the wound," McGuire wrote. "His suffering at this time was intense; his hands were cold, his skin clammy, his face pale, and his lips compressed and bloodless."

But McGuire also noted that Jackson's "complete control... over his mind, enfeebled as it was, by loss of blood, pain, etc., was wonderful."

McGuire stopped Jackson's bleeding, administered whiskey and morphine, then directed men to load Jackson onto an ambulance that just arrived. They quickly departed westward toward a makeshift field hospital.

Riding in the ambulance with Jackson was Colonel Stapleton Crutchfield, Jackson's chief of artillery, who suffered from a badly broken leg. Stapleton was, according to McGuire, "suffering intensely," groaning aloud as the wagon bumped and bounced down the Turnpike.

The morphine and whiskey kept Jackson calm and quiet, so Crutchfield didn't realize the identity of his fellow patient. When he finally asked McGuire, who told the artillerist that it was Jackson, seriously wounded, Crutchfield cried aloud, "Oh, my God!" Jackson, mistaking it for an especially acute cry of pain, asked the ambulance to halt so that something could be done to relieve Crutchfield's suffering.

Behind them, to the east, the two snarling armies continued to shoot lightning and thunder at each other through the thick woods and darkness. Before them, to the west, the field hospital still lay miles away down the Turnpike.

The full moon lit their way.

The India-rubber raincoat Jackson wore on the night of May 2.

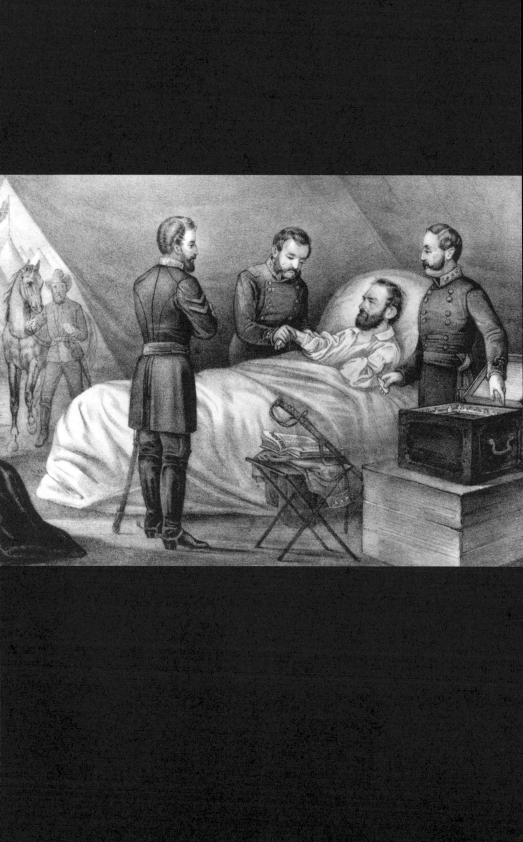

CHAPTER THREE

THE OPERATION

Sunday, May 3, 1863

Jackson at the Wilderness field hospital following the amputation of his left arm.

Nearly two and a half hours passed before McGuire could do a thorough examination. During that time, the ambulance had arrived at the field hospital located just beyond the Wilderness Tavern. Dr. Harvey Black, the surgeon in charge there and McGuire's second-in-command, offered his tent for Jackson's treatment.

"Several of us were sitting around the fire and one boy remarked jestingly that a tent had been put up for Gen'l Jackson, that he had fought so well that we could afford to Give him one," John Samuel Apperson, a steward at the field hospital, wrote in his diary. "Another said he was wounded— Had his leg shot off. He did not mean it—several of us laughed at the idea of Jackson being wounded—knowing that he had escaped in so many hard fought battles."

The mood at the field hospital quickly shifted when word spread about the true extent of Jackson's injuries. "[T]he truth is too painful to write," Apperson noted.

By two o'clock a.m., Jackson had stabilized enough that McGuire could conduct his examination. "I informed him that chloroform would be given him, and his wounds examined," McGuire later wrote. "I told him that amputation would probably be required, and asked if it was found necessary, whether it should be done at once."

"Yes, certainly," Jackson replied. "Doctor McGuire, do for me whatever you think best."

As the doctor administered the chloroform, Jackson

Alexander Swift "Sandie" Pendleton, member of Jackson's staff.

exclaimed, "What an infinite blessing," repeating that last word over and over as he drifted into a semi-conscious stupor.

The surgical team first removed the round ball from Jackson's right hand. McGuire confirmed that the bullet came from a "smooth-bore Springfield musket"—in other words, friendly fire. McGuire gave the bullet to Lieutenant James Power Smith, one of Jackson's staff officers, who later gave the bullet to Mrs. Jackson.

Next, the team amputated Jackson's left arm two inches below the shoulder. Jackson would later claim that he heard "the most beautiful music" while under the effects of the anesthesia—the music of the bone saw cutting through his shattered limb.

The surgeons' work concluded in just under an hour.

*　　*　　*　　*　　*

News came in from the battlefield that General Hill, who'd assumed command after Jackson's wounding, had also been injured. General Stuart, who had never before led an infantry corps, was now in command. He sent word back to Jackson, asking for any guidance the general might be able to offer; "Sandie" Pendleton served as the courier.

McGuire, at first, resisted any attempts to disturb Jackson's rest. Pendleton persisted. McGuire relented. However, as Pendleton explained the situation in detail to Jackson, Jackson struggled to concentrate. "Say to General Stuart that he must do what he thinks best," Jackson finally said.

Jackson slept for several hours and, when he awoke, seemed to feel better, although by mid-morning he complained of pain in his side. McGuire, examining him, couldn't detect any problems. "[T]he skin was not broken or bruised," he said, "and the lung performed, as far as I could tell, its proper functions."

Word of Jackson's wounding eventually reached General Lee. "Any victory is dearly bought that deprives us of the services of General Jackson even for a short time," Lee said.

The commander dashed off a dispatch to Jackson, which arrived at the field hospital later that morning. "I cannot express my regret at the occurrence," Lee wrote of Jackson's injury. "Could I have directed events, I should have chosen for the good of the country to have been disabled in your stead... I congratulate you upon the victory which is due to your skill and energy."

"General Lee is very kind," Jackson said, "but he should give the praise to God."

At that point in the battle, though, victory was anything but assured. May 3 would prove to be the bloodiest morning of the Civil War. Stuart would succeed in linking his wing of the Confederate army back up with Lee's wing, sustaining some sixty-five hundred casualties in the process. Soldiers of the Second Corps would cry "Remember Jackson!" as they fought.

The Stonewall Brigade, in particular, would acquit itself well. "The men of that command will be proud one day to say to their children, 'I was one of the Stonewall Brigade,'" Jackson would say when told of their performance. "I have no right to the name 'Stonewall.' It belongs to the brigade and not at all to me."

The 18th North Carolina also fought well on May 3. The nearly 325 men in the regiment sustained 126 casualties: thirty killed and ninety-six wounded. "Remember Stonewall!" they cried as they threw themselves into battle.

Despite their tenacity, though, the 18th North Carolina would never be able to erase the stigma of being the unit that shot Stonewall Jackson. As the war would continue, so would the 18th's poor luck. By Appomattox, the regiment would lose three battle flags and their commander, Brigadier General James Lane, would never advance beyond his current rank even though he demonstrated gallantry and strong leadership in later battles, and even as younger, less experienced and less capable men got promoted around him.

Jackson's wounding would haunt Lane. Not only had Jackson been Lane's corps commander, he had once been Lane's professor at VMI and later a faculty colleague. "There are periods in every man's life when all the concentrated

Jackson's handkerchief, stained with his own blood.

sorrow and bitterness of years seemed gathered into one short day or night of agony," Lane said after the war:

Though victory was assured, imagine my feelings as I lay all black with soot and smoke under an oak reckoning the fearful cost; and reflected, that in less than forty eight hours one third of my entire command had been swept away, one field officer, only, left fit for duty out of thirteen carried into action—the rest all killed or wounded— most of them being my warmest friends; my boy brother who had been on my staff lying dead on the field; and Stonewall Jackson, my old professor, whom as a boy I had not fully appreciated and whom, as my commanding officer, I dearly loved, lying mortally wounded and probably dying, shot by my own gallant command, those brave North Carolina Veterans whom I had so often heard wildly cheering him as he appeared on many a battle field.

The Union army, meanwhile, fared worse on May 3 than their Confederate counterparts. They would sustain twelve thousand casualties during the day's fighting. One of those casualties would be "Fighting Joe" Hooker himself, who would be knocked senseless by an exploding cannonball on the front porch of the Chancellor mansion.

Demoralized and defeated, Hooker would ignore the advice of some of his best generals and withdraw his army back across the Rappahannock River to safety.

But all that lay in the future. As May 3 unfolded, the situation seemed anything but certain. Lee sent word to McGuire that Jackson must be moved farther away from the front to avoid any risk of capture.

"If the enemy does come, I am not afraid of them," Jackson said. "I have always been kind to their wounded, and I am sure they will be kind to me."

He would not get the opportunity to find out. McGuire made plans to transfer Jackson twenty-seven miles by ambulance to Guiney Station, where Jackson could catch a train to Richmond and convalesce there in complete safety. Their first leg of the trip, on Monday, May 4, would take them to Fairfield plantation, home of the Chandler family. The rail line ran literally through the Chandlers' back yard.

Lee, in the meantime, spent a great deal of time thinking about Jackson, but the demands of command prevented him from seeing his fallen lieutenant.

"Give General Jackson my affectionate regards," Lee would say to Jackson's preacher, the Reverend Beverly Tucker Lacy. "Say to him: He has lost his left arm, but I have lost my right.

"Tell him to get well and come back to me as soon as he can."

"GIVE GENERAL JACKSON MY AFFECTIONATE REGARDS....TELL HIM TO GET WELL AND COME BACK TO ME AS SOON AS HE CAN."

—*General Robert E. Lee to Reverend Beverly Tucker Lacy.*

CHAPTER FOUR

THE PLANTATION

Sunday, May 3, 1863

The Fairfield plantation grew a variety of crops, including corn and, pictured here, tobacco.

With the undecided battle still raging to the northwest, hundreds of wounded soldiers already blanketed the lawns and fields around Guiney Station, waiting for the trains that would take them south to the hospitals of Richmond.

Nestled away in northern Caroline County, Fairfield had been owned by Thomas Coleman Chandler, one of the wealthiest men in the county. Chandler had sold Fairfield in March of 1863 but was staying on—and would continue to do so until March of 1865—to serve as custodian until the property transfer concluded. Until then, he would take care of Fairfield as well as his new home, Ingleside, three miles away.

In his sixties and on his second marriage, Chandler had five daughters, one stepson, and three sons, all three of whom served in the Confederate Army as part of the 9th Virginia Cavalry. Chandler had stayed home from the war to oversee the 744-acre plantation—a reasonably large estate for the time—and its sixty-seven slaves.

Over the course of the summer of 1862, though, the number of slaves dwindled slightly because of the presence of Union soldiers occupying nearby Fredericksburg. Chandler filed a grievance with the local justice of the peace, claiming that eight of his slaves "were induced away, and abducted by the army." He estimated the value of the slaves at $10,550. He lost fourteen cattle as well, valued at $600. "[T]he said slaves, nor any of the cattle have not been returned," the court papers complained.

The Fairfield office, photographed sometime prior to 1880.

The incidents would be Fairfield's first direct brush with the war.

* * * * *

Fairfield was one of four Chandler plantations that sat adjacent to one another along the Ni River Valley: Fairfield, Spring Grove, Nyland, and West Wood. Together, they totaled more than twenty-five hundred acres. Most of the property was sown with corn and tobacco, although it yielded other crops as well. Chandler also kept a fair amount of livestock. Chandler's slaves provided the work force, although Chandler himself frequently worked the fields alongside them.

At the heart of the plantation, Chandler, his second wife, Mary, and six children lived in a modest two-story brick home. The house had an attic and a half-basement, where the kitchen and dining room were located. There was a large first-floor parlor with folding doors that could subdivide the space in half. The house had chimneys on the north and south ends and a small porch adorning the front, which overlooked a carriage road. The back door overlooked three terraced gardens where vegetables, herbs, and flowers grew.

The grounds around the main house also included stables,

a tobacco barn, a goat barn, slave quarters, and a white-frame office building constructed in 1828 by the plantation's previous owner. The office had two front doors, and the left door had a roofed porch. Two chimneys rose from back of the structure, and a small lean-to had been built around one of them. Inside, an entrance hall led visitors to three downstairs rooms, with a stairway leading up to two more.

In the 1850s, part of the office had been used by Thomas Chandler's son, Dr. Joseph Chandler, for his medical practice, but by the time war broke out, Joseph had moved his practice to his own plantation and the office building had been converted entirely to plantation use.

Nearly 100 yards behind the plantation office building lay the tracks of the Richmond, Fredericksburg, and Potomac Railroad, the lifeline for prewar Fredericksburg and, during the winter of 1862-63, the Army of Northern Virginia.

Guiney Station served as the rail line's northernmost supply depot; farther north, the railway came too close to the Union line for safe transport. The rail station in Guiney had originally been established in 1836. The following year, the RF&P extended its track farther north to Fredericksburg. From there, stagecoaches took goods to the mouth of Aquia Creek on the Potomac River, where they could be taken by barge upriver to Washington.

The railroad depot at Guiney Station served as the railhead for the Confederate army, which made it the logical point of departure for Jackson, who would be transported south to Richmond for recovery.

Guiney got its name from an 18th Century Irish family that had lived in the area. Their name, spelled variously as "Ginney" and "Guinney" in colonial-era records, eventually evolved into "Guiney" and ultimately "Guinea." In fact, the alternative spellings of Guiney/Guinea continued for decades until an arbitrary decision by the local post office codified the modern spelling as "Guinea." Today, visitors can still see a multitude of spellings on street signs, buildings, and roadside markers as they drive through the area.

But no one was passing through Guiney Station on May 3, 1863. Union cavalry had torn up the rail tracks to the south. Trains weren't moving. The wounded weren't being evacuated.

And the most important patient of all would soon be on his way.

CHAPTER FIVE

THE ARRIVAL

———————

Monday, May 4, 1863

The ambulance pulled up to the Chandler property around 8:00 p.m. Stretcher bearers would carry Jackson into a room prepared for him in the small white office building.

They lined the road to watch him pass.

Twenty-seven miles, through Spotsylvania then Caroline counties, the ambulance wound over small hills and down small dips, around curves and over streams.

Along the way, people stood on the roadside to catch a glimpse of the great general or to pay their respects. Some of them brought, as gifts, hams and freshly baked bread. "[A]long the whole route, men and women rushed to the ambulance, bringing all the poor delicacies they had," McGuire later recalled, "and with tearful eyes they blessed him, and prayed for his recovery."

Mapmaker Jedediah Hotchkiss led the way, plotting out the route to Guiney Station on maps he himself had made. Hotchkiss, now thirty-four, had joined Jackson's staff in the spring of 1862, and when Jackson had ordered him to "Make me a map of the Valley," the resulting work played a key role in Jackson's string of victories there. A native New Yorker, Hotchkiss had settled in the Valley in his late teens and established an academy where he served as principal. He took up cartography, geology, and engineering merely as hobbies but quickly established a reputation as one of Virginia's most notable experts in those fields.

As Hotchkiss mapped out the route to Guiney Station, engineers traveled with him, clearing rocks and logs out of the way to make the ambulance ride smoother. "We passed crowds of wounded men going the same way," Hotchkiss would write, "all cheerful and each one wishing himself the badly wounded one instead of General Jackson."

The walking wounded were not the only ones on the road. "[R]ough teamsters sometimes refused to move their loaded wagons out of the way for an ambulance, until told that it contained Jackson," McGuire wrote, perhaps with a tinge of hyperbole, "and then, with all possible speed, they gave the way, and stood with hats off, and weeping, as he went by."

For his part, Jackson stood the ride well. McGuire rode along with him in the ambulance, as did James Power Smith and Rev. Lacy. Stapleton Crutchfield, doing much better, also rode along for part of the way. Crutchfield lived at a nearby plantation called Snow Hill. At Spotsylvania Court House, Crutchfield's uncle met the ambulance train and took the wounded colonel home to recuperate.

At the rear of the ambulance train, the responsibility of managing the horses, the headquarters supplies, and Jackson's personal effects fell to the able Jim Lewis. Lewis was a black man—probably a slave—who'd joined the staff in the fall of 1861 when Jackson was still stationed in Winchester. Information on Lewis remains incomplete, but records suggest he may have belonged to William C. Lewis of Rockbridge County, near Jackson's hometown of Lexington, and that Jackson may have hired Lewis out for about $12.50 per month.

In the postwar years, the image of "the faithful slave" willingly serving the Confederate cause would become a contrived stereotype used for political purposes. In reality, most slaves who worked for the Confederacy did so because they were either forced to or, in Lewis's case, because they were hired to, not because of a sense of political or patriotic duty. One Confederate commented that a slave could earn as much as ten dollars a week if he attached himself to an officer in the army—a considerable sum, since most soldiers made thirteen dollars a month.

Yet Lewis did serve, too, out of personal duty. He was exactly the kind of hard-working, God-fearing man Jackson had always surrounded himself with, and a genuine affection and devotion existed between the two men. Lewis had also earned the esteem and respect of everyone on the headquarters staff. McGuire remembered Lewis as "brave" and "big-hearted," as well as professional. "God bless him!" McGuire wrote.

And so, for fifteen hours, with Hotchkiss in the lead and Lewis bringing up the rear, the procession cautiously traced the route the mapmaker laid out, south and east, south and east. McGuire noted with some encouragement that Jackson "remained cheerful throughout the day" and was "disposed to converse on common subjects." Lacy, too, noticed how well Jackson seemed to be doing. "[H]e made no complaints and maintained his unfailing courtesy in answer to all inquiries, saying he felt far more comfortable than he had a right to expect," Lacy said.

Jedediah Hotchkiss, Jackson's mapmaker.

At one point, Jackson suffered a slight bout of nausea. Jackson believed in hydropathy—that water, applied properly, had medical benefits—so he asked McGuire to place a wet towel over his stomach. When McGuire complied, Jackson expressed his "great relief."

On they went.

*　　*　　*　　*　　*

Twelve-year-old Lucy Chandler sat with her mother on the front porch of her home. Inside, the harsh thump of boots on wooden floorboards and the moans of sick and injured officers and the murmur of conversation and of hushed words of succor all chased away any hope for a quiet moment. Even outside, with thousands of wounded soldiers spread out on the fields around the house, little opportunity existed for mother and daughter to share a moment of peace, but it would have to do.

Their reverie didn't last long. Sometime around four p.m., a courier arrived to inform Mrs. Chandler that General Jackson was on his way, by ambulance, badly wounded. Mrs. Chandler quickly directed that the downstairs parlor be converted into a bedroom for Jackson. However, when

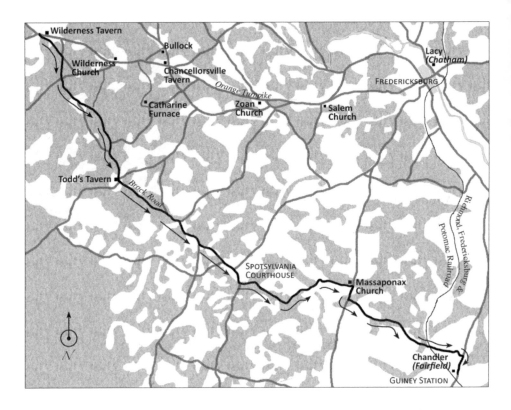

Route of the ambulance that carried Jackson to Guiney Station.

Rev. Lacy arrived for a look around, he knew the accommodations wouldn't do. The din created by all the other occupants of the house would make it impossible for Jackson to convalesce in peace. McGuire specifically insisted on quiet.

At Lacy's prompting, Mrs. Chandler took him outside to the white frame cottage that sat next to the house and usually served as the plantation's office building. At the moment, though, it remained unoccupied. With its large entryway, three downstairs rooms, and two upstairs rooms, the building had plenty of space to accommodate Jackson and his entourage until a train could transport them south. One room even had a bed in it already, a four-poster that Lucy would later describe as "a bedstand of the old-fashioned kind that you wind up with a rope."

Lacy returned to the ambulance train while Mrs. Chandler oversaw the conversion of the cottage.

The day's warm temperatures gave way to a chill as evening came on. Scattered showers swept through the area. Darkness settled in.

It was eight o'clock in the evening when Mrs. Chandler, from the window of the main house, spotted the lanterns of a wagon party crossing the railroad tracks. Her husband, Thomas, stood next to the fence that ran out front along the driveway and waited to greet them.

Jackson, exhausted, still retained his manners and composure when he saw his host. "I am sorry I cannot shake hands with you," Jackson said, "but one arm is gone and my right hand is wounded."

McGuire took the opportunity to inspect the office building, which met his approval. A quick inspection of the main house confirmed Lacy's initial impression, but McGuire also found an additional reason to keep Jackson out: Signs of an infection abounded inside the house. Jackson had to remain isolated from the illness at all costs.

The move into the office building didn't take long, and soon Jackson was resting comfortably in the bed. He took a meal of bread and tea, which he ate "with evident relish," McGuire reported, and then the patient settled down for a good night's sleep.

He slept well the night through.

"I AM SORRY I CANNOT SHAKE HANDS WITH YOU, BUT ONE ARM IS GONE AND MY RIGHT HAND IS WOUNDED."

—Stonewall Jackson to Thomas Chandler

CHAPTER SIX

THE RECOVERY

Tuesday, May 5–
Wednesday, May 6, 1863

Outside the room where Jackson rested.

While his patient slept, McGuire kept vigil. All night long, he stayed awake to monitor his patient's progress.

No one, he ordered, was allowed to disturb Jackson. No one was even allowed in the room without McGuire's explicit permission. Aside from himself, only Smith, Lacy, and Lewis had free access to the room, but they all needed rest almost as much as Jackson. They'd all been awake since the start of the flank march on the morning of the second, some three days earlier.

Smith initially occupied one of the upstairs rooms; fellow staff officer Lieutenant Joseph Morrison, away on special assignment, would share the room when he returned. Lewis took the room next to Jackson's so he'd be readily available should McGuire need an extra pair of hands, although he would eventually move upstairs as well.

Their patient made it through the night without any difficulty. Jackson awoke on the morning of Tuesday, May 5, feeling well rested.

"I found his wounds to be doing very well to-day," McGuire wrote. "Union...had taken place, to some extent, in the stump, and the rest of the surface of the wound exposed, was covered with healthy granulations"—another word for "scabbing."

His right hand, which the smoothbore bullet had lodged in, gave Jackson some pain, but "the discharge was healthy," and McGuire pronounced his satisfaction with Jackson's overall progress. The doctor applied lint and water dressings to

James Power Smith, one of Jackson's most trusted aides.

both wounds and put "a light, short splint" on Jackson's hand.

Jackson "expressed great satisfaction when told that his wounds were healing," McGuire later recalled, "and asked if I could tell from their appearance, how long he would be kept from the field."

"Many would regard them as a great misfortunate," Jackson said of his wounds. "I regard them as one of the blessings of my life."

Smith, who was on hand, responded with a favorite Bible passage: "All things work together for good to them that love God."

"Yes, that's it," Jackson replied. "That's it."

The two men, joined by Lacy, passed much of the day talking about theology. Jackson passed much of Wednesday with the two men in much the same way.

"[H]e greatly enjoyed religious conversation," his wife, Mary Anna, would later write, recalling stories Smith and Lacy had passed on to her. "During the few days succeeding his fall, when he and his friends were buoyed up by the hope of his recovery, he conversed freely and cheerfully, and expressed a desire to be taken, as soon as he was able, to his beloved home at Lexington, where, he said, the pure, bracing mountain air would soon heal his wounds and renew his strength and health."

Still, McGuire decided to ask for a consultation, and an ideal candidate happened to be relatively close: Dr. Samuel Morrison, a medical school classmate of McGuire's who currently served as the chief surgeon for Brigadier General Jubal Early's division. Morrison, a cousin of Mary Anna's who hailed from Rockbridge County, had served as the Jackson family's physician prior to the war.

Morrison arrived, at McGuire's request, on the afternoon of May 5. "That's an old familiar face," Jackson said, greeting his kinsman warmly. After pleasant chit-chat, Morrison examined Jackson and eventually confirmed McGuire's diagnosis. McGuire asked Morrison to remain with him on site; the doctor agreed.

Jackson napped on and off throughout May 5 and 6. At one point on Tuesday, Jackson awoke from an opiate-

During his convalescence, Jackson and his staff members spent a great deal of time discussion religious matters and reading Bible passages.

induced sleep and began to call to his adjutant, Sandie Pendleton: "Major Pendleton, send in and see if there is higher ground back of Chancellorsville."

Overall, though, Jackson continued to show signs of improvement, and he expressed optimism about his condition. "Although he had avowed his perfect willingness to die whenever God called him, he believed that his time was not yet come, and that God still had a work for him to do in defence [sic] of his country," Mary Anna wrote.

On May 6, rain pattered on the roof overhead. Jackson napped throughout the afternoon. Although he didn't have much of an appetite, his vital signs seemed stable and his condition slightly better. McGuire expressed optimism. "He eat [sic] heartily, for one in his condition, and was uniformly cheerful," McGuire said.

As the evening of May 6 wore on, McGuire felt confident enough about Jackson's condition that he allowed himself the luxury of a nap. The doctor had been awake for three straight days. McGuire stretched out on the fainting couch that had been brought into the room, and he drifted off to sleep.

For his patient, though, the night would prove to be the most difficult night yet.

The Reverend Beverly T. Lacy.

CHAPTER SEVEN
THE MISSION

— • —

Sunday, May 3 —
Thursday, May 7, 1863

Mary Anna Morrison Jackson. While most of Jackson's staff accompanied the general as he made his winding way by ambulance toward Guiney Station, one staff member proceeded toward a different destination. Lieutenant Joseph Morrison was on his way to find his sister, Mary Anna—General Jackson's wife.

Mary Anna had been with the army only a few weeks earlier. On a rainy Monday, April 20, Mary Anna had arrived at Guiney Station with her five-month-old daughter, Julia, and Julia's nurse, Hetty. For the first time, Jackson met his newborn daughter. "[H]is face was all sunshine and gladness," Mary Anna remembered, "and, after greeting his wife, it was a picture, indeed, to see his look of perfect delight and admiration as his eyes fell upon that baby!"

The nine days Mary Anna and Julia stayed with Jackson were among the happiest in his life. They stayed at Belvoir, a beautiful hilltop home owned by Thomas Yerby, just a mile down the road from the farm where Jackson kept his headquarters.

"During the whole of this short visit, when he was with us, he rarely had her out of his arms, walking her, and amusing her in every way that he could think of—sometimes holding her up before a mirror and saying, admiringly, 'Now, Miss Jackson, look at yourself!'" Mary Anna remembered. "When she slept in the day, he would often kneel over her cradle, and gaze upon her little face with the most rapt admiration, and he said he felt almost as if she were an angel...."

MARY ANNA LATER
SAID SHE PREFERRED
THE FIRST PHOTO,
THE WINCHESTER
PORTRAIT, TAKEN IN
THE SPRING OF 1862,
BECAUSE HER HUSBAND
LOOKED LESS STERN
AND HAD "THE BEAMING
SUNLIGHT OF HIS
HOME-LOOK."

On April 23, the couple had their daughter baptized by Rev. Lacy. On April 26, they attended church service with General Lee. "I was somewhat awe-struck at the idea of meeting the commander-in-chief..." Mary Anna wrote, "but I was met by a face so kind and fatherly, and a greeting so cordial, that I was at once reassured and put at ease."

Also during Mary Anna's visit, she persuaded her husband to sit for a photographer. "After arranging his hair myself, which was unusually long for him, and curled in large ringlets, he sat in the hall of the [Yerby] house, where a strong wind blew in his face, causing him to frown, and giving a sternness to his countenance that was not natural," Mary Anna said. The resulting photo, known as the Chancellorsville portrait, was only the second wartime photo taken of Jackson. Mary Anna later said she preferred the first photo, the Winchester portrait, taken in the spring of 1862, because her husband looked less stern and had "the beaming sunlight of his home-look."

The visit came to an end on April 29 when first news reached Jackson about Federal stirrings on the Rappahannock. "After a tender and hasty good-bye, he hurried off without breakfast," Mary Anna said. Jackson left her in the care of Rev. Lacy, who escorted her, Julia, and Hetty back to Guiney Station, where they caught the next train to the Confederate capital. There, Mary Anna found a place to stay with family friends, including James Power Smith's sister, Elizabeth Brown.

On May 3, as Jackson lay in a hospital tent recovering from his amputation and McGuire formulated plans for his evacuation to Guiney Station, the general asked Morrison to travel to Richmond and find Mary Anna. Morrison would have to break the news to her about Jackson's injury and then, as soon thereafter as practicable, escort her to Guiney Station where she could meet the ambulance party. Her presence would, no doubt, lend comfort to the general during his recuperation.

Morrison was eleven years younger than his sister. When the war broke out, he had been a cadet at VMI, but in the summer of 1862, he took an official leave of absence from the Institute to take a position on his brother-in-law's staff. Jackson expected his young relative to demonstrate "early rising, boldness, industry, and enterprise."

Now, charged with this new mission, Morrison had to demonstrate speed and compassion.

The young lieutenant left for Richmond by train accompanied by one of Governor John Letcher's aides. They made it as far as Ashland, thirty-five miles to the south, but then had to abandon the train because of threats from Union cavalry operating in the area.

As part of his grand strategy, Union army commander Joe Hooker had ordered his cavalry, under Brigadier General George Stoneman—Jackson's old West Point roommate—to get between the Confederate army and its capital and disrupt communications and supplies. The raid, in conjunction with Hooker's bold move against Lee in Fredericksburg, would send the Confederates into a panicked retreat. Of course, things had gone terribly wrong for Hooker who, by the afternoon of May 3, was crumbling under Confederate pressure.

Stoneman had no way to know that Hooker's plan had unraveled, so he and his four thousand men continued their raid. In the end, his efforts would be about as unsuccessful as Hooker's turned out to be, but on May 3, his mere presence did plenty to upset Confederate equilibrium.

At one point, Stoneman's cavalry captured Morrison's train and nearly captured Morrison himself, but the young lieutenant and his companion eluded detection by jumping from the train and hiding in a forest. They eventually found a pair of horses, and the two men rode the rest of the way into the city. In all, it had taken Morrison three days to reach his destination.

Meanwhile, on Sunday, Elizabeth Brown's husband, the Reverend William Brown, had heard that Jackson had been wounded during the battle. He broke the news to Mary Anna following worship service that morning. "This painful shock can be better imagined than described," Mary Anna later said. "Despatches were sent at once inquiring into his condition, and asking if I could go to him. He was reported as doing well, but the way was not open for me to come yet. The

Joseph G. Morrison, Jackson's brother-in-law and a member of his staff.

raiding-parties of the enemy were operating all through the intervening country."

Although Mary Anna was willing to risk the danger, the Browns persuaded her to wait. "[N]o tongue or pen can express the torturing suspense and distress of mind which I endured during this period of enforced absence from him," she said.

When her brother finally arrived, he did much to assure Mary Anna that her husband was "thought to be doing as well as possible" and "was brave and cheerful in spirit."

"Everything was said and done to cheer and encourage me, but oh, the harrowing agony of that long waiting, day after day!" Mary Anna said.

By Thursday, Confederate engineers repaired Stoneman's ineffectual attempts at railroad wrecking. Mary Anna, Hetty, and Julia again made the trip north, this time under Morrison's escort. Governor Letcher joined them, as well. "During all this long period of anxiety and suspense," Mary Anna wrote of her daughter, "my unconscious little nestling was all sweetness and sunshine, shedding the only brightness and comfort over my darkened pathway."

Their trip, in an armored railroad car, lasted a few uneventful hours. They arrived in Guiney Station at around noon. James Power Smith met them at the station.

"How is my husband?" Mary Anna inquired almost immediately.

"Pretty well," Smith answered, although his tone and manner betrayed him.

Mary Anna's heart, she later said, "sank like lead."

Compounding her anxiety was the fact that she wasn't allowed in to see her husband just yet. Doctors were changing his bandages, Smith explained, and they had asked everyone to wait outside.

Mary Anna tried to walk off her impatience on the piazza of the main house. She passed the time by making lemonade for her husband. The time felt like hours, she said, although she knew her wait couldn't have been long.

Just then, a party of gravediggers not a stone's throw from the house caught her eye. From the pit, they exhumed a coffin—that of Brigadier General Frank Paxton, she would later learn, a friend from Lexington who had died during the battle of Chancellorsville while leading the Stonewall Brigade.

"My own heart almost stood still under the weight of horror and apprehension which then oppressed me," Mary Anna recalled. "This ghastly spectacle was a most unfitting preparation for my entrance into the presence of my stricken husband."

But then the summons came, and Mary Anna entered the small white office building. Even the shocking sight of the gravediggers hadn't prepared her for what she saw when she entered her husband's room.

"[T]he sight which there met my eyes," she wrote, "was far more appalling, and sent such a thrill of agony and heart-sinking through me as I had never known before!"

"EVERYTHING WAS SAID AND DONE TO CHEER AND ENCOURAGE ME, BUT OH, THE HARROWING AGONY OF THAT LONG WAITING, DAY AFTER DAY!"

—Mary Anna Jackson

CHAPTER EIGHT

THE LAST DAYS OF STONEWALL JACKSON

Thursday, May 7– Sunday, May 10, 1863

The bed in which Jackson spent the last few days of his life.

On Wednesday night, confident that Jackson was resting comfortably, McGuire had finally allowed himself to drift off into a much-delayed and much-needed sleep. As the doctor slept, Jim Lewis had stepped in to keep a vigilant eye on Jackson. All seemed well.

Silence filled the room, broken only by the ticking of the clock on the fireplace mantel.

But shortly after one a.m., Jackson's sleep became fitful. He began to moan and gasp. Lewis immediately appeared at Jackson's bedside. Rev. Lacy joined him.

They found Jackson feverish and nauseated. He felt a sharp pain stabbing through his side, he told them. That pain had bothered him on and off since his fall from the litter during his evacuation from the battlefield, but McGuire had examined the injury and had seen no obvious problem. Jackson suggested to Lewis that a wet compress, such as the one McGuire had approved during the ambulance ride from the battlefield, might do the trick; after all, it had worked then.

Shouldn't they wake McGuire? Lewis and Lacy both asked.

No, no, Jackson told them. The doctor needed his sleep. Just get the wet compress and see if that does the trick.

It didn't. The pain worsened as the night dragged on. By daylight, Jackson breathed in agony. He finally consented to let Lewis and Lacy wake McGuire.

The doctor, concerned to find Jackson in such poor shape,

"reproved Mr. [Lacy], right harshly," about the unauthorized hydropathy. Jackson had to assuage him. "[T]he General, knowing that I had slept none," McGuire later said, "refused to allow the servant to disturb me, and demanded the towel."

A brief examination revealed the worst. Jackson suffered from "pleuro-pneumonia" on the right side. Initially, McGuire attributed the pneumonia to internal injuries sustained in the fall from the litter. "Contusion of the lung...was probably produced by the fall," McGuire would later write, "and shock and loss of blood prevented any ill effects until reaction had been well established, and then inflammation ensued."

Indeed, Jackson's fall from the litter may have resulted in pleurisy, which made his side ache and his breathing so difficult. The resulting inflammation and build-up of fluid around the lungs, McGuire reasoned, led to the pneumonia. Both conditions probably contributed to Jackson's spells of fever.

In the years since, McGuire's diagnosis has been a source of much speculation and second-guessing. It wasn't until the 1990s that research revealed that McGuire was not privy to all the facts of the case. For instance, McGuire didn't realize Jackson had complained of chills on May 1 and 2, or that Jackson had slept on the ground the night of May 1. Despite temperatures in the eighties on May 2, when Jackson undertook the flank march he wore every article of clothing he owned, including his heavy India-rubber raincoat. Such insights now suggest Jackson was sick before he was ever even wounded and that the trauma of Jackson's injuries masked the extent of his illness.

The rumor mill of 1863 churned out its own speculations. A popular one centered on Lacy's unauthorized hydropathy. "[T]his gave rise, probably, to the report that the pneumonia was induced by wet cloths," McGuire later grumbled. "The disease came on too soon after this application to admit of the supposition."

As McGuire tried to make sense of his patient's worsening condition, he knew he'd need help. Although he had Dr. Morrison on hand, he decided to also send word to other physicians who might be able to assist, particularly Dr. David

Tucker of Richmond, a leading expert on pneumonia. McGuire also asked for consultations from Drs. J. Philip Smith and Robert Breckenridge.

In the meantime, McGuire resorted to "cupping," a medical procedure that involved placing hot golf ball-sized glass cups on Jackson's skin. The hot glass would cause the skin to blister, thus drawing excess fluids to the surface of the body where they could be lanced and expelled. McGuire also applied hot mustard wraps, and he administered mercury, antimony, and opium. The idea was to use the antimony and mercury to purge Jackson's system by inducing vomiting and diarrhea. Unfortunately these "medications," which were much more like poisons, may have done more harm than good. The drugs dulled Jackson's sensitivity to pain, but they also dulled his senses, acted as depressives, and affected his heart rate and breathing.

A wick ran from a bowl of water at Jackson's bedside to the bandages wrapped around the stump of his left arm. The wet bandages were easier to change. Doctors also thought the moisture facilitated healing.

As morning wore into afternoon, and the treatments continued, Jackson asked for a glass of lemonade. Smith, trying to make himself useful, brought a glass in for the general. This was the lemonade Mary Anna had mixed shortly after her arrival.

"You did not mix this," Jackson said to Smith after taking a sip. "This is too sweet. Take it back." Only his wife mixed lemonade so sweetly—and indeed, that's when Jackson realized his wife had arrived.

Mary Anna stood in the doorway of the room, transfixed by her husband's "fearful wounds, his mutilated arm, the scratches upon his face, and, above all, the desperate pneumonia, which was flushing his cheeks, oppressing his breathing, and benumbing his senses...."

Jackson, under the influence of laudanum, still managed a smile. "I am very glad to see you looking so bright," he said. "My darling, you must cheer up and not wear a long face. I love cheerfulness and brightness in a sickroom."

He called her his esposita, his little sweetheart, a term he had picked up during a stay in Mexico City at the end of the Mexican War. "You are one of the most precious little wives in the world," he told her.

At various times, McGuire and Mary Anna both stole quick naps on a couch in Jackson's room.

The drugs soon regained their hold on Jackson, and he faded back into unconsciousness. "From the time I reached him he was too ill to notice or talk much," Mary Anna later said, "and he lay most of the time in a semi-conscious state; but when aroused, he recognized those about him and consciousness would return."

And so the rest of the afternoon passed, with Jackson drifting back and forth between consciousness, delirium, and sleep. "He breathed badly, suffering much pain & at times was delirious," wrote Dr. Morrison. From his dreams, Jackson would shout out, reliving scenes of battle. He called for General A. P. Hill. He called for his commissary officer, Major Wells Hawks. He called for the infantry to move forward.

Overall, though, the day of rest seemed to do Jackson some good. Toward evening, McGuire noted that his patient's condition had improved. He said, "[H]opes were again entertained of his recovery."

*　　*　　*　　*　　*

Jackson slept little that night, but Dr. Morrison noted that "Friday morning was better" and that Jackson "seemed nearly

McGuire and his team of medical experts tried every treatment they could think of to try to arrest the deepening pneumonia.

wholly relieved from pain & his mind in a much better condition." McGuire found more reason for optimism when he again dressed Jackson's wounds. "The process of healing was still going on," he said. The pain in Jackson's side had disappeared, too.

But not all was entirely well, McGuire noted: Jackson "breathed with difficulty and complained of a feeling of great exhaustion."

By day's end, Dr. Morrison found Jackson's "delirium more constant, & his strength failing tho when his attention was called, seemed to recognize all persons present, & understand every thing spoken to him." Jackson repeatedly told the doctors that "he suffered very little pain, & believed he would be better soon."

Mary Anna seldom left her husband's bedside except to go to Julia. At one point, near the end, she brought the baby in, which elicited a delighted smile from her husband. "Little darling! Sweet one!" he said, calling the child his "little comforter." He watched her intently, "with radiant smiles," then he closed his eyes and raised his hand over her, committing her to God. "Though she was suffering the pangs of extreme hunger, from long absence from her mother, she seemed to

Doctors huddled in the room next to Jackson's, trying to plot out a course of treatment.

forget her discomfort in the joy of seeing that loving face beam on her once more," Mary Anna later recalled. "She looked at him and smiled as long as he continued to notice her."

Mary Anna, Rev. Lacy, and other members of Jackson's staff all prayed with Jackson during those few days. They read Bible verses and sang hymns, including one based on Psalm 51, which Jackson had treasured as one of his favorites:

Show pity, Lord; O Lord, Forgive;
Let a repenting rebel live;
Are not thy mercies large and free?
May not a sinner trust in thee?

Meanwhile, McGuire and his team of doctors tried everything they could to counteract the pneumonia—but to no avail. "I see from the number of physicians that you think my condition dangerous," Jackson told McGuire on Saturday, May 9, "but I thank God, if it is His will, that I am ready to go. I am not afraid to die."

By that evening, Jackson's fever and restlessness had increased, and "although everything was done for his relief and benefit, he was growing perceptibly weaker," Mary Anna noticed.

McGuire quietly admitted that recovery looked hopeless.

On the morning of Sunday, May 10, Dr. Morrison, kinsman and family physician, broke the news to Mary Anna. "[T]he doctors, having done everything that human skill could devise to stay the hand of death, had lost all hope," Mary Anna later recalled. "[L]ife was fast ebbing away, and they felt that they must prepare me for the inevitable event, which was now a question of only a few short hours."

Mary Anna needed a few moments to collect herself from the "stunning blow." She realized, she told Dr. Morrison, that she had to break the news to her husband. He would want to know. He would want the time to prepare himself.

"This was all the harder," Mary Anna wrote, "because he had never, from the time that he first rallied from his wounds, thought he would die, and had expressed the belief that God still had work for him to do, and would raise him up to do it."

Mary Anna reentered Jackson's room and took her position at his bedside, praying for the strength to hold her composure. Jackson appeared to be sinking fast into unconsciousness, but Mary Anna's voice, when it finally came, seemed to rouse him.

"Do you know the doctors say you must very soon be in Heaven?" she asked.

At first, Jackson did not seem to understand, so Mary Anna repeated her question. After making much effort to shake off his stupor, Jackson finally replied: "I prefer it."

"Well," she told him, "before this day closes, you will be with the blessed Saviour in His glory."

Mary Anna finally broke down. She fell across the bed and bitterly wept.

After she calmed, Jackson called for McGuire. "Doctor, Anna informs me that you have told her I am to die today," he said. "Is it so?

McGuire confirmed it was, indeed. Jackson looked to the ceiling for a moment, as if in intense thought. "Very good," he finally said. "Very good. It is all right."

* * * * *

A clock on the mantel ticked away Jackson's last hours.

The clock on the fireplace mantel ticked by the day's slow minutes.

Jackson told Mary Anna he had so much he wanted to say to her but was too weak. They did manage to discuss some of his last wishes, where he wanted to be buried, where he wanted her to go after his death.

Members of Jackson's staff came in for final interviews. Many of them wept openly. Sandie Pendleton cried so hard he had to excuse himself and walk outside. Jim Lewis sobbed inconsolably. "Tears were shed over that dying bed by strong men who were unused to weep, and it was touching to see the genuine grief of his servant, Jim, who nursed him faithfully to the end," Mary Anna wrote.

Jackson maintained a peaceful demeanor throughout, due in large part to the drugs but also due to the strength of his faith. "It is the Lord's day," he said at one point. "My wish is fulfilled. I have always desired to die on a Sunday."

McGuire offered Jackson some brandy and water, but Jackson demurred. "It will only delay my departure, and do no good," the general said. "I want to preserve my mind, if possible, to the last."

At army headquarters, where the Reverend Lacy conducted a prayer service, some 1,800 soldiers attended. Afterwards, General Lee took the chaplain aside. "When you return, I trust you will find him better," Lee said. "When a suitable occasion offers, tell him that I prayed for him last night as I never prayed, I believe, for myself."

But Lacy would not return to Fairfield in time.

By three o'clock, Jackson had slipped entirely into delirium. Distraught by his patient's condition, McGuire would excuse himself from the room—"unable in my enfeebled condition to restrain my grief at seeing him die," he later admitted in a private letter to a friend.

From his deathbed, Jackson called out more battle orders. "Push up the columns," he ordered. "Hasten the columns! Pendleton, you take charge of that! Where's Pendleton?

Tell him to push up the columns! Order A.P. Hill to prepare for action! Pass the infantry to the front rapidly! Tell Major Hawks—"

He stopped in mid-sentence, and his countenance relaxed. Witnesses noted that a "smile of ineffable sweetness spread itself across (Jackson's) pale face" and his voice softened "as if in relief."

Quietly, Jackson said, "Let us cross over the river, and rest under the shade of the trees."

And then the thirty-nine-year-old Jackson died.

In that moment, even the ticking clock on the mantel would hold its clockwork breath. McGuire would stop its swinging pendulum, would freeze that instant of time, to mark the time of death.

"Without pain," said McGuire, "or the least struggle, his spirit passed from the earth to the God who gave it."

QUIETLY, JACKSON SAID, "LET US CROSS OVER THE RIVER, AND REST UNDER THE SHADE OF THE TREES."

—*The last words of Stonewalll Jackson*

CHAPTER NINE

THE FUNERAL

Monday, May 11–
Friday, May 15, 1863

Mary Anna and Julia visit Jackson's grave.

The Lexington Presbyterian Church, where Jackson served as a deacon prior to the war.

Mary Anna awoke that night bathed in the light of the half-full moon. "[A]ll in my chamber was perfect stillness," she noted. Next to her, Julia slept quietly.

The enormity of the previous day's events weighed on Mary Anna, who later recalled "the agony and anguish of those silent midnight hours." She despaired, she grieved, she wept—and finally, through prayer, she found peace.

The next morning, she visited her husband's body, which lay in state in the parlor of the Chandlers' main house. Spring flowers lined the casket, and lilies of the valley wreathed Jackson's face. His staff members, who had overseen the preparation of the body, had clothed him in ordinary dress and then wrapped him in a dark blue military overcoat. His Confederate uniform had been too badly damaged on the night of his wounding.

Later that morning, the journey to Richmond began. A special railcar transported Jackson's coffin, his family, his staff, and a few attendants. Virginia Governor John Letcher also joined them. In the city's northern suburbs, the governor's wife, Susan Letcher, and a group of mourners met the train and escorted Mary Anna to the governor's mansion while the train, with Jackson's body, moved onward. Mrs. Letcher wanted to spare Mary Anna the distress of a public arrival in the city.

Flags in the capital flew at half-staff. Businesses closed. Throngs of people lined the railway. "The whole city came

Mourners visit Jackson's grave.

forth to meet the dead chieftain," wrote one observer. "Amidst a solemn silence, only broken by the boom of the minute guns and the wails of a military dirge, the coffin was borne into the governor's gates, and hidden for a time from the eyes of the multitude, that were wet with tears."

Officials draped Jackson's coffin with the "Stainless Banner," the newly adopted national flag of the Confederacy, a white rectangular field with the well-known St. Andrew's cross "battle flag" design in the upper-left corner. The flag would later become known as the "Jackson flag."

On Tuesday, a full military procession transported Jackson's coffin to the capitol building for a public viewing. A team of white horses pulled the hearse, followed by a party of Confederate officers, led by Lieutenant General James Longstreet, acting as official pallbearers.

Behind them came Jim Lewis and one of Jackson's mounts, Superior, standing in for the beloved but missing Little Sorrel, captured by the Union army following his dash through the woods and into enemy lines on the night of May 2. Only weeks before, Jackson had playfully shown off Superior to Mary Anna during her visit to Belvoir, whizzing across the lawn so fast his hat flew off. Now, the great chestnut stallion plodded along solemnly, empty boots facing backwards, fastened in his stirrups.

Jackson lay in state in his former VMI classroom. Today, a statue of Jackson stands in front of the building.

Behind Superior followed Mary Anna and Julia, Governor Letcher and President Jefferson Davis, and a host of other officials and dignitaries. Even a few members of the Stonewall Brigade had come for the procession.

Some twenty thousand mourners filed past the casket as it lay in the capitol. Women who passed the bier placed flowers on it. Soon, the bier and the table it rested on "overflowed with piles of these numerous tributes of affection," Mary Anna noted.

Early on Wednesday, Jackson's coffin was returned to the governor's mansion for a private memorial service and then, from there, taken to the rail depot. The funeral party traveled by train to Gordonsville and then on to Lynchburg. All along the route, crowds assembled to pay their respects.

At Lynchburg, Jackson's casket was transferred to a canal boat, the *Marshall*, which then ferried the party on the last leg of its journey to Lexington. When it arrived on Thursday evening, a large crowd awaited. "[O]ur pastor...and our friends and neighbors met us in tears and sorrow," Mary Anna wrote.

In 1891, Jackson's remains were removed from their original resting place and reinterred at the foot of a new bronze statue at the center of the cemetery. The monument was unveiled on July 21—the thirtieth anniversary of the First Battle of Manassas.

The corps of cadets from the Virginia Military Institute, guided by Superintendent Francis Smith, took charge of Jackson's casket, which they transported to the VMI campus, to Jackson's former classroom, Room 39. He had taught in that room for ten years; now he would spend one final night there. Some of his former pupils stood guard.

"First in the heart of the brave men he has so often led to victory, there is not a home in the Confederacy that will not feel the loss and lament it as a great national calamity," Smith had told the cadet corps. "But our loss is distinctive. He was peculiarly our own.... Reverence the memory of such a man as General Jackson."

Late into the night, mourners filed into the classroom. Flowers were piled so high they reportedly hid the casket.

"He left the Va. Military Institute in command of the Cadets," wrote the *Lexington Gazette*. "He has been brought back to sleep among us—a world renowned Christian hero."

*   *   *   *   *

The next day, May 15, dawned mild and clear. Temperatures in the Valley that day would peak at seventy degrees. At VMI, the artillery pieces Jackson had so long commanded boomed every half hour throughout the morning, falling silent when the funeral procession left the campus at ten a.m.

The procession wound from VMI to downtown Lexington, where some four thousand people crammed in and around the Presbyterian church where Jackson had served as a deacon prior to the war. The service, conducted "amid the flowing tears of a vast concourse of people," featured remarks and eulogies from several pastors, including Dr. William F. Junkin, the brother of Jackson's late first wife, Ellie.

Rev. James B. Ramsey, in his eulogy, spoke of Jackson's "noble character" and "bright example" and described Jackson as "eminently a happy man, cheerful and free...just as kind, as gentle and as tender, as he was stern and inexorable in his requirements when duty and the interests of his country demanded, and as he was lion-like in battle." Ramsey pointed to Jackson's faith as "the source of that quiet daring, that lofty heroism, that imperturbable coolness and self possession, even in those sudden and dangerous emergencies which wound up all his energies to their utmost tension, that made him the model soldier, the true Christian hero."

The main eulogy came from Dr. William S. White, who had served as Jackson's spiritual counselor since Jackson's early days in Lexington. Fewer men had impacted Jackson's life as significantly. Jackson had seen himself as a soldier of God and White as his commanding officer. In his eulogy, White read excerpts from the many letters Jackson had sent to him from the front. White also quoted from 1 Corinthians 15: "The last enemy that shall be destroyed is death."

Following the service, the procession flowed southward to the cemetery. Jim Lewis still led the horse, the boots in the stirrups still reversed.

Jackson was laid to rest, with full military honors, in a shady plot next to his eldest daughter, Mary Graham, who'd been born in 1858 and had lived only a few weeks. Nearby lay Jackson's first wife, Ellie, who had died giving birth to their stillborn son, buried with her.

All things considered, though, Mary Anna considered it a beautiful spot: "the gentle eminence commanding the loveliest views of peaceful, picturesque valleys, beyond which, like faithful sentinels, rise the everlasting hills."

Margaret Junkin Preston, sister to Jackson's first wife and a dear friend of Jackson, was among those at the service. "Now it is all over," she wrote in her journal, "and the hero is left 'alone in his glory.' Not many better men have lived and died."

"BUT OUR LOSS IS DISTINCTIVE. HE WAS PECULIARLY OUR OWN.... REVERENCE THE MEMORY OF SUCH A MAN AS GENERAL JACKSON."

–VMI Superintendent Francis Smith

CHAPTER TEN
THE ARM

May 3, 1863

James Power Smith erected a monument for Jackson's arm in 1903.

And then there was the matter of Stonewall Jackson's arm.

While Jackson was buried in his hometown of Lexington, his amputated left arm remained in a burial plot of its own, one hundred miles to the east, just beyond the Chancellorsville battlefield, where it had been laid to rest on May 3 by Rev. Lacy.

Lacy had come that day to visit Jackson as soon as he had heard about the general's wounding. When he arrived at the field hospital, he broke into tears when he saw the extent of Jackson's injury. "Oh, General, what a calamity," he cried.

Lacy and Jackson had formed a close bond during their six months of service together. The two had known each other in Lexington before the war, although for the four years prior to the conflict, Lacy had been pastor for the Presbyterian congregation in Frankfort, Kentucky. He had moved to Fredericksburg in 1862, then to Orange Court House, where he served wounded soldiers. In January of 1863, Jackson asked Lacy to oversee the chaplain service of the entire Second Corps.

Lacy was ideally suited for the position. Born in 1819 to a clergyman father in Prince Edward County, Virginia, Lacy eventually went on to Washington College and Union Theological Society. Mary Anna called him a true "spiritual comforter."

But on the morning of May 3, it was Jackson providing the comfort, meager as it was in his weakened condition. He consoled his friend, and when the time finally came for Lacy to depart, they parted on an optimistic note. Lacy would

Rev. Beverley Tucker Lacy's brother owned a plantation, Ellwood, that sat only a mile from the Wilderness field hospital where Jackson's arm had been amputated.

spend a great deal of time with Jackson over the next seven days, and he would serve as the principal messenger bringing communications from Lee. It would be Lacy to whom Lee would say, "He has lost his left arm, but I have lost my right."

As it happened, that left arm was much on Lacy's mind. He found it, wrapped in a cloth, outside Jackson's tent, where the doctors had placed it following the operation. Worried that it would end up as one of many on a pile of amputated limbs eventually destined for a mass, unmarked grave, and convinced that it deserved a better fate, Lacy collected Jackson's arm and determined to dispose of it in a more fitting manner.

Lacy set out northeast across the fields toward the nearby home of his brother, J. Horace Lacy. Lacy's home, called Ellwood, had been built around 1790. Lacy assumed owner-ship in 1848 when he married the daughter of the building's original owner. The plantation grew corn, wheat, and oats, tended by several dozen slaves. However, the Lacys primarily used Ellwood as a summer home; they also owned a larger home in Fredericksburg, Chatham, which overlooked the Rappahannock River.

James Horace Lacy, the brother of Rev. Beverley Tucker Lacy, Jackson's chaplain

Rev. Lacy laid Jackson's arm to rest in the family cemetery.

Later, Mary Anna was asked if she wanted the arm exhumed and buried with her husband in Lexington. "Was it given a Christian burial?" she asked. Assured that it was, she consented to let the arm remain at Ellwood.

Not that the arm necessarily rested in peace. When Union forces occupied the area in May of 1864, they dug up the arm and, satisfied that it was really there, reburied it.

Popular legend also has it that United States Marine Corps General Smedley Butler, in the area for a Marine Corps exercise in 1921, excavated the arm and then reburied it, in a metal ammunition box, with full military honors. That story, which has taken on a life of its own, probably never happened. The Marines did, however, place a plaque on the side of the arm's monument: "A Tribute to the Memory of Stonewall Jackson by the East Coast Expeditionary Force: United States Marines Sept. 26-Oct. 4, 1921."

The monument itself was placed there by an intimate of Jackson's who sought to preserve the general's memory: James Powers Smith.

A TRIBUTE TO THE MEMORY
OF
STONEWALL JACKSON
BY THE
EAST COAST EXPEDITIONARY FORCE
UNITED STATES MARINES.
SEPT. 26 – OCT. 4, 1921.

The Marine's expeditionary force mounted a plaque on the granite marker in 1921.

After the war, Smith had married Agnes Lacy, Horace's oldest daughter, and went on to a successful career as a Presbyterian minister for a church on the corner of Princess Anne and George streets in Fredericksburg. Smith always kept an eye on the grave of his beloved commander's arm. In 1903, as one of ten granite markers Smith placed around the area's battlefields, he installed the marker at the cemetery. It reads "Stonewall Jackson's arm—Buried May 3, 1863." Fifteen members of the Lacy family lie interred in the cemetery, but only Jackson's arm has a marker.

Still, Stonewall Jackson's arm is not the only limb in United States military history with its own unique story. Major General Benedict Arnold, who would go down in U.S. history as a notorious turncoat for switching his allegiance to the British during the American Revolution, has a monument for a lost limb. At the 1777 Battle of Saratoga, while still serving the American cause, Arnold led a brilliant charge against a British position, but British musket balls tore apart his left leg, which was then crushed under his fallen horse. The monument, erected in 1887 near Freeman's Farm, depicts a bas-relief boot, but the monument's inscription refers only to the memory of "the most brilliant soldier" in the army without naming Arnold by name because of his subsequent infamy.

During the Mexican War, at the battle of Cerro Gordo, the 4th Illinois Infantry captured the cork leg of Mexican General Antonio Lopez de Santa Anna. The Illinois National Guard has kept the leg as a trophy, displaying it at its museum in Springfield.

Another leg, this one belonging to flamboyant Union officer and politician Major General Daniel E. Sickles, remains in the possession of the Army Medical Museum in Washington, D.C. Sickles lost his left leg in the Peach Orchard on the second day of the Battle of Gettysburg. In a show of bravado as he was being carried off the battlefield, Sickles smoked a cigar and ordered that his dismembered leg be saved. He later sent it to the museum, which pickled it and put it on display. Sickles would visit his leg at least once a year for the rest of his life.

"FIFTEEN MEMBERS OF THE LACY FAMILY LIE INTERRED IN THE CEMETERY, BUT ONLY JACKSON'S ARM HAS A MARKER."

CHAPTER ELEVEN

THE VISITORS

May 21, 1864

Lieutenant General Ulysses S. Grant, photographed during the Overland Campaign of 1864.

He'd been at the Confederates for weeks, an almost continuous grind through the tangles of the Wilderness, the trenches of Spotsylvania, and the rain and mud of spring. Now the thrust-and-parry was on anew, this time in a race to the North Anna River, the next major obstacle on the Union Army's inexorable march toward Richmond.

Ulysses S. Grant needed a few minutes to just sit.

Fairfield provided a much-needed repose for Grant, who sat on the front porch of the Chandler house, smoking a cigar and thinking. His aide, Captain Horace Porter, sat with him. The plantation's lawns and fields, stretched out before them, bore the marks of a skirmish earlier in the day between the advancing Federal army and the 9th Virginia Cavalry—the unit, ironically, that Thomas Chandler's sons served in.

The day had been warm, and it had been long, and Grant had only made it as far as Guiney Station. The lead elements of the army had passed through some thirteen hours earlier, dangled in advance like bait. Robert E. Lee had not pounced on it. Now Grant, with the rest of the army, was trying to close up ranks so that those lead elements didn't remain so vulnerable.

With the day winding down, Grant's staff had first pitched his tent near the home of Edmund Motley—"an elderly man of a certain sour dignity," wrote a Union staff officer, "a bitter rebel plainly." Grant rarely impinged on a homeowner by making his headquarters in their house, but

GRANT HAD EVEN KNOWN JACKSON AT WEST POINT, ALTHOUGH NOT WELL—GRANT'S LAST YEAR AT THE POINT COINCIDED WITH JACKSON'S FIRST.

he sometimes appropriated space on their front porch to sit in a rocking chair, smoke a cigar, and think. A few moments of peace and quiet at the end of the day let him collect his thoughts.

But when ashes from Grant's cigar burned the armchair and flickered onto Motley's porch, Motley erupted. You're trying to burn down my house, the old man cried.

Grant decided to find another porch—one less noisy and bothersome.

And so he and Porter had walked to the next plantation over, to Fairfield, and had found a comfortable chair where he could smoke and think in peace.

Grant and Porter sat there several minutes before the front door swung open and Mary Chandler stepped out. The men rose to their feet, removed their hats, and bowed.

At the time, Grant was the second-most-powerful man in the United States and, as a lieutenant general, the highest-ranking army officer since George Washington. Mrs. Chandler, ever the socialite, knew how important he was. With all her powers of Southern hospitality, she charmed Grant and Porter, treating them like friendly neighbors who'd just stopped by for a chat.

It didn't take long for the conversation to turn toward the little white office building that sat to the right of the main house. Mrs. Chandler gave the men a tour. "This house has witnessed some sad scenes," she told them. "One of our greatest generals died here just a year ago—General Jackson—Stonewall Jackson of blessed memory."

Grant told her that he and Jackson had served in the same army during the Mexican War. Grant had even known Jackson at West Point, although not well—Grant's last year at The Point coincided with Jackson's first.

"Then you must have known what a great and good man he was," Mrs. Chandler said.

"Oh yes," Grant conceded, "he was a sterling, manly cadet, and enjoyed the respect of everyone who knew him." Grant then praised Jackson's "indomitable energy" as a student.

"He was a gallant soldier and a Christian gentleman," Grant

730.   General Grant's Council of War.
[FOR DESCRIPTION OF THIS VIEW SEE THE OTHER SIDE OF THIS CARD.]

concluded, "and I can understand fully the admiration your people have for him."

Jackson's death, just over a year past, still seemed to strike Mrs. Chandler particularly hard. As she continued her conversation with Grant and Porter, she "became very much affected," Porter later recalled, "and almost broke down in recalling the sad event."

But Grant was no longer looking backwards; he was looking ahead—toward the North Anna River, toward Richmond, toward Robert E. Lee and the Army of Northern Virginia.

It was time, he knew, to get back to business.

Grant thanked Mrs. Chandler for her hospitality, and he told her he would post a guard to protect her property, then he and Porter politely took their leave.

As it turned out, they would be the first of many tourists who would stop at the little white building to pay their respects.

General Grant's council of war, held at Massaponax Church while en route to Guiney Station on May 21, 1864. Grant, standing left with his back to the camera, leans over Meade's shoulder to study a map.

CHAPTER TWELVE

THE DECLINE

May 1864 — August 1903

The first effort to memorialize the place where Jackson died came when James Power Smith placed a granite marker on the property.

On May 10, 1863, James Power Smith had stood by Jackson's bedside as his commander passed away. His service to Jackson remained a source of pride and profound meaning to the young man. As he grew older, and as the nation's war scars began to heal, he decided to commemorate some of the significant wartime events that had taken place around his adopted hometown of Fredericksburg. With funding from a wealthy Virginia admirer, Smith commissioned the placement of ten markers around the area's battlefields.

The first marker, placed in August of 1903, sat down the slope from the white office building at Fairfield, facing the rail line that connected Richmond with Fredericksburg and points north. Approximately three feet high and made of granite, the marker simply stated, "Stonewall Jackson Died: May 10, 1863."

At the crest of the hill, serving as a sad backdrop to the marker, Fairfield stood as an empty shell of its former splendor. In the forty years that had elapsed since Jackson had passed away, Fairfield had passed into its own decline.

First, the plantation had changed owners. The farm had been sold in 1863, apparently against the better wishes of Mary Chandler. She seemed to cling onto the farm as long as she could, and she and her husband may have even stayed on for a while as caretakers—but by March of 1865, the Chandlers were off to their new home, "Lake Farm," located

Above and Right:

In the years after the war,

Fairfield fell into decline.

just down the road. Thomas Chandler was ready to try his hand at managing his new property.

The Chandlers stayed at Lake Farm only five years before moving again, this time to a newly constructed house Thomas Chandler christened "Ingleside," which sat less than three miles from Fairfield. Chandler would live out his remaining days there, passing away in 1890 at the age of 92. Mary, meanwhile, passed away in 1881 at the age of 62.

When the Chandlers sold Fairfield, ownership fell to Dr. Edgar McKinney of Richmond, who bought several properties around Guiney. For a time, he and the Chandlers were the major landholders in the area. McKinney did not own the farm long, though. He died in the 1870s, and the land was then parceled out and sold to various parties. The once-thriving plantation, encompassing more than 740 acres, was whittled down to a fraction of its former size. Many of the buildings had fallen into disrepair. The once-fertile land was worn from years of agricultural production.

The few photographs that still exist of Fairfield during that period between its purchase by McKinney and the placement of Smith's marker show an increasingly shabby shack.

The whitewash looks grimier. The trees and shrubs look wilder. A few tobacco plants look exhausted. The windows stare like hollow eyes.

"If one could project the bleak pictures backward..." wrote historian Ralph Happel, "we should have a Currier and Ives model of a solid rural seat, a picture of Victorian tranquility in the summer sun, showing posed in happy pursuits a household unmindful of change and sad tales of dying generals."

But by 1903, even though Smith's marker commemorated the great events that had happened there, Fairfield was dying, too.

James Power Smith, later in life, erected a memorial to mark the spot where his beloved commander died.

CHAPTER THIRTEEN

THE RESTORATION

1909 — The Present

The National Park Service
undertook a major renovation
of the Shrine in the 1960s.

In the spring of 1864, William White was among the 257 cadets and six officers from the Virginia Military Institute called out to face a Union army sweeping down the Shenandoah Valley. Across the fields of New Market, with lightning breaking open the sky above them, the cadets charged into battle at a critical juncture, helping to turn the tide in favor of the Confederates.

In the years that followed, White would graduate from VMI and eventually take a faculty position there. Later, he would take a job with the Richmond, Fredericksburg, and Potomac Railroad. By 1903, he was serving as the RF&P's president.

White never forgot his VMI roots, though—or VMI's greatest hero.

In August of 1909, when he heard that Fairfield was slated for sale at auction, White bought five acres of the property, including the main house and, more importantly to White, the small office building where Stonewall Jackson died.

What was left of the plantation had fallen into disrepair. The last known picture of the farm shows a dry, almost barren landscape devoid of its former lush vibrancy. In the office building, Jackson's room had turned into a basket weaver's shop; wood shavings littered the floor. The adjacent tobacco and goat houses were in dire need of repair. The main house, in worst shape of all, teetered on collapse. A fire, reputedly sparked by lightning, had ravaged it in 1902.

When the railroad owned the building, PR-savvy officials made sure passengers saw the attraction as their trains passed by.

White had little interest in the main house, though, and had the remains torn down. His conservation efforts focused on the ramshackle office building and the property overall. In 1913, he purchased another 7.13 acres and also began restoration work on the office.

As part of his effort to memorialize Jackson, and as a way to entertain passengers, White made a special effort to promote the building's location in RF&P's literature. On the hillside facing the railroad, White installed a bed of white gravel and, in letters made of English boxwood, planted the legend "In this house Stonewall Jackson died May 10 1863."

White donated the property to the railroad in 1911, and in 1919 the railroad installed a caretaker on the grounds. That same year, the railroad opened the property to the public.

In 1927, a group of private citizens—including Lucy Chandler, whose parents had owned the plantation when Jackson died there—began a rehabilitation effort that included interior furnishings and rugs. A key furnishing, the bed in which Jackson died, remained in the possession of the Museum of the Confederacy, which had acquired the piece in 1900 through the efforts of Hunter McGuire. The Museum agreed to turn over the bed when the restoration project wrapped up.

To go with the bed, several Chandler great-grandchildren donated one of several blankets used to cover Jackson when he'd been in the bed. A third piece, perhaps the most dramatic, was donated by none other than Lucy Chandler herself: the clock, which had sat on the fireplace mantel and ticked away Jackson's last days.

The room where Jackson died got an overhaul as part of the NPS renovation in the 1960s.

As part of the publicity efforts surrounding the rehabilitation project, the name "Stonewall Jackson Shrine" first appeared. Virginia Lee Cox, a reporter for the *Richmond Times-Dispatch,* coined the term in a report published on November 16, 1926.

As momentum grew for the rehabilitation efforts, the RF&P announced financial backing that would make an even more extensive renovation possible. As part of the project, the railroad removed the white stones and boxwood letters.

On October 12, 1928, the Stonewall Jackson Shrine had its official dedication. A newspaper editorial called it "a place where lovers of history and heroism might journey and worship."

While the word "shrine" often implies a location of religious significance, a more antiquated meaning of the word made "shrine" a synonym for "museum." The Jamestown colony in Virginia, for instance, was long called the Jamestown Shrine before the National Park Service folded it into what is now Colonial National Historical Park. Downtown Fredericksburg, Virginia, boasts two shrines: the James Monroe Shrine, devoted to America's fifth president, and the Hugh Mercer Apothecary Shop, billed as "a museum of Early American Pharmacy and as a shrine for the organized pharmacists of the United States."

Renovation efforts included adding a lean-to back on to the Shrine. Part of the original structure, the lean-to had been removed in the early part of the twentieth century.

The National Park Service, when it accepted possession of the Stonewall Jackson Shrine from the railroad in 1937, kept the building's name since it intended to maintain the structure as a museum. "In commemorating (Stonewall Jackson), we pay homage to those qualities which he so well exemplified," said Charles West, acting secretary of the Interior, during the rededication ceremony: "Manhood, integrity, and honor, virtues that know no sectional lines, that command respect everywhere."

* * * * *

While the name has remained the same, the Shrine has seen a number of other changes, some small and some significant. The route of the driveway has changed several times before finally settling into the path it follows today, which closely traces a road cut by the Confederates in 1863.

On the exterior of the Shrine, a side porch was added and later removed. Shrubs have been planted and removed. A windmill, built over the old well, towered over the Shrine for a spell. James Powers Smith's granite marker has skipped across the property from location to location, unburdened by the extra words added in the 1970's: "Buried in Lexington,

VA." The additional line had been added because visitors frequently mistook the monument for Jackson's tombstone.

The biggest changes to the property came during a massive restoration project initiated by the National Park Service in 1963. The building was stripped and restored to its appearance from one hundred years earlier. A lean-to on the back of the building, which had been removed by the 1890s, was added back on. The three-quarter shutters installed by Thomas Chandler, intended to protect privacy while still letting in some sunlight, were recreated. Renovators added modern fire-suppression and environmental-control systems. Carpenters replaced the roof.

Over the years, James Power Smith's granite marker has been moved to various spots on the property.

Forty-five percent of the exterior and nearly seventy-five percent of the interior consists of original materials. The floor in Jackson's room, the stairs leading to the second floor, the window casings, and the fireplaces, for instance, are all original.

Even many of the non-original materials in the building have an historical connection to the story of Jackson's death. The floorboards in the entryway, for instance, come from a barn, built in 1828—the same year as the Shrine—on the nearby Catlett Farm on Locust Hill. Panes of rippled window glass come from Ormsby, a nearby plantation.

The rest of the property today consists of a caretaker's house tucked for privacy behind a row of tall shrubs, a restroom facility, and a few interpretive signs. A marker points out the former location of the main Chandler house. Along with the half-dozen apple trees near the rear of the Shrine, a dozen or so older, taller trees dot the front and side yards. In all, the National Park Service has preserved a significant amount of land around the site: more than fifty acres.

A carpenter examines his handiwork during renovation efforts.

And near the parking lot, Smith's granite marker, quiet and unobtrusive, continues to catch the eyes of visitors. Smith, a principal actor in the drama that unfolded in the Chandlers' office building, was the first to commemorate those events. Now, thousands of visitors come to the Shrine each year to do the same.

CHAPTER FOURTEEN

THE SHRINE

————•—•————

Today

The Stonewall Jackson Shrine. They come from all over the world, from places like Bellmore, New York, and Lubbock, Texas; Charlottesville, Virginia, and Hampden, Maine. They come from places like Jackson, Mississippi, and Jackson, Michigan, and Jacksonville, Florida. They come from as far away as Iceland and Thailand and from as close as Caroline and Spotsylvania counties.

Some come because their pilgrimage has brought them here to pay reverent tribute to their fallen hero. Some come because they've heard of Stonewall Jackson and want to know what all the hullabaloo is about. Some come because it's just a short hop off the interstate, where the roadside sign happened to catch their eye and pique their curiosity: What is the "Jackson Shrine," anyway? Why is it here, in this obscure and lonely place?

But whatever has brought them here, wherever they've come from, the clock on the fireplace mantel tok-tik-tok-tik-tok-tiks for them the way it did for Jackson. They hear the same sound, from the same clock, that Jackson heard as he lay in bed during his last days.

Visitors stand in that room, pressed against the wooden railing, and marvel at that bed and listen to that sound, and some of them, the lucky ones, get swept back in time for a few moments. Sometimes, they cry.

*   *   *   *   *

One of the most famous early visitors to the Shrine was David Lloyd George, the former British Prime Minister. On a 1923 visit to America, George made a special trip to the building. "That old house witnessed the downfall of the Southern Confederacy," he said. "No doubt the history of America would have to be rewritten had 'Stonewall' Jackson lived."

But at the time of Jackson's death, history had yet to be written, and people—North and South—wondered what the impact of Jackson's death would be. Jackson's death was not only an intimate, personal tragedy for Mary Anna and Julia, it was a national tragedy, as well. "The nation indulges a personal grief," said Rev. James Ramsey in his eulogy of Jackson. "Never perhaps did such a throe of agony pierce a nation's heart."

"We feel that his death is a national calamity," wrote Colonel Abram Fulkerson of the 63rd Tennessee Infantry in

The announcement of Jackson's death in *The New York Times*.

The Death of Stonewall Jackson.

In the death of Stonewall JACKSON, the rebels have unquestionably lost by far their greatest military leader, in the peculiar style of strategy which has made his name famous. Immediately after the secession of Virginia he appeared on the scene, and ever since then he has been one of the foremost figures. He was the leader in the first hostile act of the Secessionists of Virginia—the march upon Harper's Ferry. In the first great action of the war, the battle of Manassas Plains, he took part, and one of his characteristic personal and military qualities, expressed in his title of "Stonewall," here first appeared. In every great battle fought since that time by the main rebel army, and in many minor affairs, he has been a leading actor—in the Peninsular battles, where he was the first to attack our right; in the second battle of Manassas; at the battle a letter to his wife on May 18. Fulkerson was a former student of Jackson's at VMI. "The poorest soldiers among us appreciated his worth—loved the man, and mourn his loss."

"Seldom has a people manifested so deep and universal a sorrow as that which has spread over the land with the announcement of the loss of the loved and trusted leader 'Stonewall' Jackson,'" wrote *The Charleston Mercury.*

The paper went on to say that "Though Stonewall Jackson is dead, his fiery and unequaling spirit still survives in his men. He has infused into them that which cannot die." At least one of Jackson's men, a soldier from the 37th North Carolina Infantry, wasn't so sure. "I don't think his place can ever be filled," he wrote.

The Jackson statue at Manassas: "There stands Jackson like a stone wall."

The Richmond Examiner said Jackson's loss had a greater impact on the Confederacy "than if they had lost a whole division of their army."

"[T]ho the paper is full of news," wrote North Carolina diarist Catherine Anne Devereux, she had to conclude her entry about Jackson's death because "I have no heart to write more…. I care for nothing but him…. He was the nation's idol, not a breath even from a foe has ever been breathed against his fame. His very enemies reverenced him."

Devereux hardly exaggerated, if Northern newspapers provided any indication. "Today I read the Washington papers," Confederate mapmaker Jed Hotchkiss wrote in his journal on May 15. "They all spoke highly of General Jackson, though evidently pleased that they were rid of him."

One such paper was the Daily Morning Chronicle. "While we are only too glad to be rid, in any way, of so terrible a foe, our sense of relief is not unmingled with emotions of sorrow and sympathy at the death of so brave a man," the paper said. "Every man who possesses the slightest particle of magnanimity must admire the qualities for which Stonewall Jackson was celebrated—his heroism, his bravery, his sublime devotion, his purity of character. He is not the first instance of a good man devoting himself to a bad cause." President Lincoln, after reading the piece, called it an "excellent and manly article."

**Thomas Jonathan
"Stonewall" Jackson.**

The New York Herald, in an article on May 14, called Jackson's death "a serious and an irreparable loss to the rebel army; for it is agreed on all hands that Jackson was the most brilliant rebel general generated by this war…. He was a universal favorite in the rebel armies, and popular even in our own."

Lt. John T. Norton of the 97th New York Infantry, writing to his father just days after Jackson's death, called Jackson "one of their best Generals who is a host in himself…the bravest of the brave."

That respect for Jackson in the Union army went all the way to the top, to commander Ulysses S. Grant who, during his stopover at Fairfield in May of 1864, expressed his esteem for Jackson to Mrs. Chandler.

Although "[e]verybody seemed to agree that we were having an easier time because Jackson was dead," said an officer from the 19th Maine Infantry, who'd passed through Guiney Station the same morning Grant had visited, they admitted a grudging respect for Jackson's battlefield accomplishments.

"I rejoice at Stonewall Jackson's death as a gain to our cause," said Major General Gouverneur Warren, one of Grant's corps commanders, shortly after Jackson passed away, "and yet in my soldier's heart I cannot but see him the best soldier of all this war, and grieve at his untimely death."

But because of that untimely death, as Jackson stood at the peak of his powers, his memory became enshrined in a way no other Civil War soldier—North or South—enjoyed.

"[W]e still have our 'Stonewall' in memory's heart, as he lived, fought, prayed and died…" wrote John S. Robson of the 52nd VA Infantry in his 1898 memoir. "[He] died at the precise moment of time and under the exact circumstances best calculated to perpetuate his glory and fame, which today belongs to our common country, North and South."

The Cincinnati Enquirer, in an October 1875 article, had actually taken it a step further:

In truth, the character of Stonewall Jackson lifts him above the narrow confines of State or even National limits. His military genius elevates him among the great soldiers of the world, among the select few who belong to the universal history of mankind. He was one of the few born soldiers with whom the conduct of battle was an inspiration, and whose prophetic eye always fixed upon the issue of a struggle as a certainty. Such men are too rare to be confined within the narrow pages of local history, too grand to be repressed by the weight of sectional hostility. They assert their right to universal appreciation and honor. We are rapidly approaching the point when all of us, both North and South, can honor and respect a great name, no matter on which side it came to distinction.

As a wave of commemorations swept across the country in the late 19th and early 20th centuries, statues of Jackson rose across Virginia in Richmond, in Lexington, in Charlottesville, in Manassas. One even stands atop a tall pillar in a New Orleans cemetery.

Jackson devotees, young and old, come to pay their respects.

Other memorials appeared: monuments... plaques... paintings...a stained glass window in the National Cathedral ...a manmade lake in West Virginia...schools... hospitals...roads.

West Virginia University preserves Jackson's Mill, the bucolic setting of Jackson's boyhood home, just south of Clarksburg, where Jackson was born.

In Winchester, Virginia, sitting atop the crest of a small hill is the home Jackson used as his office in the months prior to his Valley Campaign. The headquarters provides visitors with insight into a formative period of Jackson's military development.

Farther south, in Lynchburg, travelers can see the *Marshall*, the canal boat that took Jackson on the last leg of his last journey home.

The Jackson monument on the VMI parade grounds.

In Lexington, the Stonewall Jackson House on East Washington Street offers visitors a glimpse into Jackson's domestic life prior to the war. Across town, at the Virginia Military Institute, where a statue of Jackson stands at the head of the parade ground, keeping watch, visitors can learn about Jackson's academic career and visit the preserved remains of Little Sorrel. They can worship in the same

"A WONDERFUL SHRINE TO A NOBLE SOLDIER," ONE VISITOR WRITES. "A LOVELY, INTIMATE SETTING, LIKE A WALK BACK IN TIME," WRITES ANOTHER. "WE LOOK INTO OUR PAST AND SEE OUR FUTURE."

high-spired Presbyterian church where Jackson worshipped. They can visit his grave.

And, in Guinea Station, they can come to the Stonewall Jackson Shrine.

* * * * *

Perhaps they come to pay their respects or to satisfy their curiosity. Perhaps they come to enjoy the scenic beauty of the grounds.

Perhaps—as sometimes happens—they don't even know why they've come.

The Shrine, with its quiet dignity and sense of history, offers something different for everyone. The historians on duty offer an orientation and answer questions, but they like to give visitors space. The Shrine is best experienced when visitors explore at their own leisure and then ask about the things that stand out to them. Visitors may ask about the pile of rugs under the stairs (discarded from the main house, they would've been used to cover items stored in the office building) or the two birds on the bookcase in the doctors' conference room (an oriole and a pileated woodpecker, both preserved with arsenic, so they can't be handled without special gloves). They may ask about any of the artifacts scattered on any of the tables in any of the rooms. They may ask about Jackson.

They may remain silent.

Sometimes visitors ask about President Andrew Jackson (no relation to Thomas Jonathan Jackson). It's a common point of confusion. Although two generations apart, both military heroes came from the South and had famous nick-names—"Stonewall" and "Old Hickory." The historians patiently offer corrections and help visitors understand what really happened at the Shrine.

On occasion, someone with Jackson's surname will come in, claiming to be a descendant. "I'm related to Stonewall Jackson! I deserve to touch the bed," one of them demands. The general does, indeed, have living descendants, but Jackson's daughter Julia married a man with the surname Christian, so none of those descendants shares Jackson's name.

Sometimes, visitors bring flowers, or they plant small Confederate flags by the door or near the marker erected by James Powers Smith or in the grass beneath the window of Jackson's room. Sometimes, a visitor will leave a lemon or two—an offering to the spirit of a man who, as legend has it, liked to suck on fresh lemons.

Not all come to pay their respects. "I just wanted to see where the treasonous bastard died," one man growls.

Visitors jot notes in the guestbook, describing the Shrine as "Incredible, won't be forgotten"; "An honor to visit"; "fascinating"; "simple but very enjoyable"; "riveting"; "a treasure"; "just had to stop and see"; "Happy Birthday General." Many people write "interesting."

"A wonderful shrine to a noble soldier," one visitor writes. "A lovely, intimate setting, like a walk back in time," writes another. "We look into our past and see our future."

"A very surprising find."

"Still tragic and poignant to this day."

"Breaks my heart, but definitely needed to see."

"I have relived the history of a great American."

"Stonewall lives on."

Sunset at the Stonewall Jackson Shrine.

WHATEVER HAPPENED TO...?

Mary Anna Morrison Jackson

Mary Anna never remarried; she remained "The Widow of the South." She moved to Charlotte, North Carolina, where she raised Julia and was active in postwar reunions and dedications of monuments to the Confederate cause. Mary Anna did not always see eye to eye with Julia, which created tension between her and her son-in-law, William Christian. In her lifetime, Mary Anna met five presidents and lived to see the 20th Century. She died in 1915, succumbing, like her husband, to pneumonia. She is buried along with her husband and daughter in Lexington's Stonewall Jackson Cemetery.

Julia Jackson Christian

The only surviving child of Thomas and Mary Anna would live a short life. Lauded as "The Child of the Lost Cause," she cared little for the fame brought upon her by her father and mother. In 1885, she married William Christian, and the two moved to San Diego, California, perhaps to escape her controlling mother and the oppressive fame that came with being "Stonewall's daughter." The couple fell on hard times and moved back East. Julia had two children, a girl named Julia Jackson Christian (1887-1991) and a boy named Thomas Jonathan Jackson Christian (1888-1952). Like her father, Julia's life was cut short. In 1889, she contracted typhoid fever and died; she was just twenty-six years old.

Rev. Beverly Tucker Lacy

Lacy stayed with the Second Corps of the Army of Northern Virginia and after the war went on to pastor at churches in Wytheville, Virginia, and St. Louis, Missouri. He also spent time educating freed blacks in Tuscaloosa, Alabama. He retired in 1887, moving with his son to Washington, D.C. He passed away in November, 1900, and is buried in Stonewall Jackson Cemetery in Lexington.

Jim Lewis

Lewis attached himself to Sandie Pendleton, serving Jackson's former chief of staff until Pendleton's death in the fall of 1864. Jim's master did not bring him back to slavery, but little else is known of Jim after this point except that he returned to Lexington and worked in the Lexington Hotel. As legend has it, Lewis was filled with grief by the deaths of Jackson and Pendleton, which contributed to Lewis's failing health. One account states that he died in October 1864 of pneumonia while another has him living until 1866. We do know from one newspaper account that Jim died prior to 1875. He may be buried in the Lexington City Cemetery or under the Lexington Hotel.

Little Sorrel

Little Sorrel was eventually liberated from Union hands and sent to live with Mary Anna in North Carolina. Later, he was sent to VMI, where he grazed freely on the Institute's parade grounds. He was a frequent attraction at parades, veterans' reunions, and country fairs, frequently requiring a guard because of his popularity. Like other old soldiers, Little Sorrel was eventually sent to live at the Confederate Soldiers Home in Richmond, where he became a beloved pet of the veterans who lived there. Severely arthritic in his last years, Little Sorrel died in 1886 at age thirty-six. His hide was subsequently preserved and remains on display in VMI's museum. His bones were cremated and, in 1996, buried at the foot of Stonewall Jackson's statue overlooking the head of the parade grounds.

Dr. Hunter Holmes McGuire

McGuire remained with the Confederate Army until the close of the war. Afterwards, he accepted a professorship in Richmond and, while there, founded two hospitals and became a founding member of the American Medical Association. McGuire treated everyone who came to see him, even those who could not pay, and he enjoyed speaking with Confederate veterans, whom he rarely charged for his services. In 1867, he married Mary Stuart, and the couple would have ten children. In March of 1900, McGuire suffered an epileptic seizure that kept him bedridden and speechless the last few months of his life. He passed away that September.

Sandie Pendleton

Shortly after Jackson's death, Pendleton fell ill and spent time being nursed back to health in the very bed his commander had died in. He would return to service in time for the Battle of Gettysburg, but he would be killed fourteen months later, in September of 1864, at Fisher's Hill, Virginia. He is buried in Stonewall Jackson Cemetery in his hometown of Lexington.

James Power Smith

Jackson's young and loyal staff officer remained with the Second Corps of the Army of Northern Virginia. Following the war, Smith served for twenty-three years as the minister of the Presbyterian Church in Fredericksburg, Virginia. He later served as editor and owner of a Presbyterian magazine. In 1871, Smith married Agnes Lacy, whose family owned Ellwood and Chatham. The couple would have six children. Throughout his postwar years, Smith actively worked to preserve the memory of his fallen commander, including the placement of ten monuments marking the climactic events that took place around the Fredericksburg area during the Civil War. He also offered the invocation at the dedication of the Virginia Monument at Gettysburg. After forty-six years of marriage, Smith's wife died in 1916. He lived on until 1923 when, at the age of eighty-six he, too, passed away. He was the last surviving member of Stonewall Jackson's staff.

TIMELINE OF THE LIFE OF STONEWALL JACKSON

Jackson's Mill, where Jackson
grew up, near what today is
Weston, West Virginia.

1824:	Born January 21 in Clarksburg, Virginia (modern day West Virginia).
1842:	Enters the United States Military Academy at West Point.
1846:	Graduates from West Point as part of one of the most decorated classes in the school's history. Jackson ranked seventeenth out of fifty-nine.
1846-1848:	Serves in the Mexican-American War on the battlefields of Vera Cruz, Cerro Gordo, Churubusco, Contreras, and Chapultepec.
1851:	Accepts a position at the Virginia Military Institute, where he will teach Natural and Experimental Philosophy, as well as Artillery Instruction.
1853:	Marries Elinor Junkin.
1854:	In October, Elinor dies during childbirth. She is buried with their stillborn son.
1857:	Marries Mary Anna Morrison.
1858:	On February 28, Mary Anna gives birth to a daughter, Mary Graham; Mary Graham dies almost twelve weeks later on May 25.

1859:	In December, escorts VMI's Corps of Cadets for guard duty at John Brown's execution.
1860:	On December 20, South Carolina is the first of seven states to secede from the United States.
1861:	On April 17, Virginia secedes.
July 3	Jackson promoted to brigadier general in the Confederate Army.
July 21	Jackson and his brigade of Virginians receive their famous "Stonewall" nickname at the Battle of First Bull Run (Manassas) November: Jackson establishes headquarters in Winchester, Virginia.
1862:	Spring brings battle in the Shenandoah Valley. Jackson and his small army execute a fast-paced campaign of fighting and maneuvering. By the end of "Jackson's Valley Campaign," he fights and defeats three different Union armies in six different engagements, losing only one of them.
June:	Joins new army commander Robert E. Lee for the Peninsula Campaign outside Richmond. For a variety of reasons, Jackson does not perform up to standard.
August:	The new Army of Northern Virginia marches away from Richmond. Jackson wins a victory at Cedar Mountain, then drives north to Manassas, where another Confederate victory follows.
September:	Captures Harpers Ferry, the largest capture of a Union army in the war. Fights in the Battle of Antietam.
November:	Promoted to Lieutenant General and is formally given command of the Second Corps, Army of Northern Virginia. The promotion places Jackson as the third in command of the army.

December 4: Daughter Julia is born.

December 13: Fights at the Battle of Fredericksburg.

1863: In April, Jackson meets his daughter for the first time.

May 1: Jackson is ordered by Lee west toward Chancellorsville. The two men meet that night beside a fire in the Wilderness of Spotsylvania County for what becomes known as "The Crackerbox Meeting."

May 2: Jackson and Lee meet for the last time as Jackson embarks on his famous "Flank Attack" at Chancellorsville. That night, in dark woods, Jackson is accidentally wounded three times by his own men.

May 3: Jackson's left arm amputated at the Wilderness Tavern.

May 4: Taken by ambulance to Guinea Station.

May 7: Diagnosed with pneumonia. Mrs. Jackson, Julia, and Governor Letcher arrive at Guiney Station.

May 10: Jackson dies at 3:15 PM, after uttering the final words, "Let us cross over the river and rest under the shade of the tress."

May 11: Body is taken to Richmond, lies in state in the governor's mansion.

May 12: Body lies in state at the Confederate capitol.

May 13: Body begins final journey to Lexington.

May 15: Buried in Lexington, Virginia.

TIMELINE OF THE CHANDLER OFFICE BUILDING

Once opened to the public, the Stonewall Jackson Shrine became a popular tourist attraction.

circa 1670s:	Land purchased by Thornton family.
circa 1797:	Thomas Coleman Chandler born.
1798:	John Thornton inherits 465-acre tract of land, which becomes Fairfield, from his father, Colonel Anthony Thornton.
1825:	Thomas Coleman Chandler marries Clementina S. Alsop.
	John Thornton marries third wife, Mildred Washington Dade.
1828:	Thornton constructs a small office building near his main house at Fairfield.
circa 1844:	Clementina Chandler dies John Thornton dies, leaving Fairfield to Mildred.
1845:	Mildred thornton dies; Thomas Coleman Chandler buys Fairfield property from Mildred's executor.
circa 1847:	Thomas Coleman Chandler marries Mary Elizabeth Frazer (b.1819).
1850's:	Part of office building used by Chandler's son, Dr. Joseph A. Chandler, for his medical practice.
1854:	Used as a temporary home of the Chandlers during the construction of new main house.

1859:	Chandler's father-in-law, Sam Alsop, wills properties to his grandsons.
1862-63:	Dec.-Feb. Used as the headquarters of Brigadier General Fitzhugh Lee's cavalry brigade.
1863:	Mar. Fairfield Plantation is sold by Thomas Chandler to Doctor Edgar McKenney, a physician from Richmond.
May:	Used to care for General Thomas J. Jackson; Jackson's adjutant, Sandie Pendleton, would later recover there from the same sickness.
1890:	Thomas Coleman Chandler died; buried beside his wife in Spotsylvania Court House.
1890's:	Used as a basket weaver's shop.
1903:	Monument to the death of Jackson placed near the former Chandler office building.
1909:	Acquired by Richmond, Fredericksburg, & Potomac Railroad President William White.
	Brick main house torn down by William White.
1911:	Ownership of land and office building transferred to R. F. & P.
1919:	Caretaker hired to oversee site.
1920:	Grounds and office opened for tours to the public.
1927-28:	Some restoration of the building by the railroad.
1928:	"Shrine" is officially dedicated.
1937:	National Park Service accepts the Shrine as an historic structure; preliminary restoration undertaken.
1963:	Renovation by National Park Service.
2003:	Driveway paved.

ABOUT THE AUTHORS

Kristopher D. White holds a master's degree in military history from Norwich University. A former Licensed Battlefield Guide at Gettysburg, White works as a ranger/historian at Fredericksburg & Spotsylvania National Military Park (FSNMP) in Virginia.

Chris Mackowski, an associate professor of journalism and mass communication at St. Bonaventure University, has won numerous awards for his writing. He works as a historical interpreter at FSNMP.